Adding
Value

CHRISTOPHER R. PETT
4343 N. KENMORE AVE. #3
CHICAGO, IL. 60613

GERARD EGAN

Adding Value

A SYSTEMATIC GUIDE TO BUSINESS-DRIVEN MANAGEMENT AND LEADERSHIP

foreword by
BERNARD F. BRENNAN

 Jossey-Bass Publishers
San Francisco

Substantial discounts on bulk quantities of Jossey-Bass books are available to corporations, professional associations, and other organizations. For details and discount information, contact the special sales department at Jossey-Bass Inc., Publishers. (415) 433-1740; Fax (415) 433-0499.

For sales outside the United States, contact Maxwell Macmillan International Publishing Group, 866 Third Avenue, New York, New York 10022.

Manufactured in the United States of America

The paper used in this book is acid-free and meets the State of California requirements for recycled paper (50 percent recycled waste, including 10 percent postconsumer waste), which are the strictest guidelines for recycled paper currently in use in the United States.

Figure 9.2 reprinted by permission of Montgomery Ward.

Library of Congress Cataloging-in-Publication Data

Egan, Gerard.
    Adding value : a systematic guide to business-driven management and leadership / Gerard Egan.
      p. cm. — (The Jossey-Bass management series)
    Includes bibliographical references and index.
    ISBN 1-55542-542-9 (acid-free paper)
    1. Strategic planning. 2. Organizational effectiveness.
3. Leadership. 4. Creativity in business. I. Title. II. Series.
HD30.28.E33 1993
658.4'092—dc20
                                        93–2936
                                          CIP

FIRST EDITION
HB Printing   10 9 8 7 6 5 4 3 2 1   *Code 9345*

The Jossey-Bass
Management Series

Contents

Foreword

Nobody knows where business is headed—nobody can because "business" is constantly being reinvented, especially in the fast-paced, chaotic times most businesses are experiencing today. But the integrated, systematic approach to management to which Gerard Egan has introduced Montgomery Ward, and which he describes in *Adding Value,* provides managers with a unified way to understand and look at business as a whole. Gerry has helped us at Montgomery Ward understand the systematic nature of the creative strategic process necessary for success in business. His approach to business management is not made up of off-the-shelf, take-it-or-leave-it concepts and tools but is a living method that companies can use in a hands-on way.

Adding Value discusses business, organizational, managerial, and leadership effectiveness in an integrated and systematic way. We have tapped these ideas in developing the Montgomery Ward "strategic leadership triangle," which serves as a guide for our business. Strategy is the top of the triangle. Gerry has helped us to see that every manager must be a strategist. Once formulated, strategy must be tested, cascaded, sold to every associate, implemented, and fine-tuned in a never-ending cycle. After strategy, the second point of the triangle is customer service, both internal and external, which is the key driver in operations.

Every manager must be a customer-service champion. Finally, the third point of the triangle is the development of people, whom we call associates. Development of people is the key organizational driver, and every manager must be a developer of associates.

Managers — all managers — play a key role in making this strategic leadership triangle come alive. Strategy must drive everything in the organization so that the organization can effectively serve the business. Gerry's systematic approach to management has helped us cascade our grand strategy into every unit of the company. At Montgomery Ward, each of our mainline businesses and each support group has its own mission and strategy, which are developed from and linked to the planks of the grand strategy.

In addition to being a strategist, every manager must also be a leader. We need leaders throughout the company, not just in the executive office. Gerry's approach to management development has helped us realize the importance of defining the Montgomery Ward brand of leadership, which must be as hard-edged and practical as our business. Our managers have learned that leadership is not just about meeting targets but is about results, about "performance beyond the ordinary." Leadership is played out differently in the executive offices than it is on the store floor, but wherever leadership occurs, "performance beyond the ordinary" is the name of the game. The sales associate who balances customer service with stock replenishment and continually finds better ways of doing both is just as much a leader and is just as essential to strategy as the executive who develops an idea for a new business. As we have learned with Gerry's help, no business can achieve a leadership position in an industry without a critical mass of leaders at every level of the organization.

Every manager must also be an agent of change. As readers will see, the systematic, unified model for initiating and managing change that Gerry presents in *Adding Value* provides both a framework for thinking about change and a tool for making it happen. It gives a common language for discussing change and for constantly improving the business and the organization that serves it, as well as offers a pragmatic model that readers can use "on the run." At Montgomery Ward, we have made extensive use of Gerry's change model. As we moved from turnaround to growth and development mode, Gerry's model helped our managers to think more creatively and to continually tap the rich ideas of all of our associates.

Another important model in Gerry's framework is fashioning a corporate culture that serves the strategy. As *Adding Value* points out, culture is not just another box on the organization chart — culture permeates the entire business. During the hectic turnaround days at Montgomery Ward, we did not have time to think much about our culture. Now we must cultivate a culture that supports what we want to accomplish in growth and development. Gerry's approach to managing the culture — especially the "shadow side" of culture — is helping us overcome business-inhibiting assumptions, attitudes, beliefs, values, and norms within our company. Further, we've introduced the notion of the learning organization to our culture to sustain and further our creativity.

Admittedly, to have every manager be at once a strategist, a champion of customer service, and developer of people is an ideal, but there is nothing to stop any of us from working toward that ideal. Likewise, for every associate to be a partner and a learner is also an ideal, but, cynics to the contrary, ideals have helped make companies great just as they have helped make our country great. We must continue to work toward creating a critical mass of managers and associates that keep us moving toward the ideal.

Chicago, Illinois   BERNARD F. BRENNAN
February 1993   Chairman and CEO
                                                                       Montgomery Ward

*This book is dedicated
to every manager who wants to
manage more effectively
and lead more creatively—
that is, to virtually every
manager in the world.*

Preface

In 1982, Peters and Waterman's book *In Search of Excellence* kicked off a period of consciousness-raising about business and organizational excellence. Like the human potential movement of the late 1960s, the excellence-in-business literature has ushered in the "business and organizational potential" movement. The basic premise is the same — most companies and institutions use only a fraction of their potential. If they were more creative and better managed, they could be much more than they are now.

There are literally hundreds of books that offer suggestions for managing more effectively. Some of these offer substance, while others offer fad and fashion — the latest idea, the most novel technique, the most current guru. It is not that many of the ideas are not good, that the techniques do not work, or that the gurus do not provide a compelling vision of what companies would look like were they to get their act together. Indeed, managers are faced with an embarrassment of riches, and therein lies the problem — which ideas are the right ones to implement?

Notwithstanding this embarrassment of riches in management models, methods, techniques, and skills, many studies (as well as simple observation and common sense) suggest that managers do not manage very well. Mismanagement is usually cited as one of the main reasons that companies fail. Mismanagement is also cited for the tremendous waste of resources by our public institutions. If so many ideas for better management are available, why do managers not use them more often? The fault lies principally not with managers but with the entire *system* of management. Managers are not the culprits; rather, they are the victims of the ways in which companies choose and develop their managers. Consider the following:

- Managers are often chosen to manage because they are good at something else—accounting, engineering, finance, merchandising.
- Companies and institutions seldom provide managers with a model or system for managing.
- Companies have no system for preparing upcoming managers for their future role. Even MBA programs, as effective as they may be in preparing managers for certain dimensions of the business—accounting, finance, marketing, or whatever—do not prepare managerial hopefuls to manage.
- Once chosen, managers are given little or no orientation, development, or training in managing.
- The managerial role itself, together with the expectations that go with it, is often ill defined.
- Managers are not forewarned about the chaotic nature of day-to-day managing. Whatever training they are eventually given—often in terms of isolated seminars on such topics as time management—is too little too late.
- Although managers are expected to produce results by working with and through the members of their team, often they are deficient in interpersonal skills, and nothing is done to remedy these deficiencies. It is no wonder, then, that supervised employees complain about "lousy managers."
- Once in the job, managers receive little guidance and little feedback on their performance.

This kind of management system is not effective. Although each company has its store of managerial wisdom into which newly appointed managers tap, little is done to improve the system as such. While it is easy to see the deficiencies of individual managers, the deficiencies of the system — or, more accurately, the nonsystem — are more difficult to perceive. Moreover, since the company next door or the competitor in the next city has the same system, it is also difficult to see that reforming the management system would constitute a distinct competitive edge.

It is time to do something about the ineffective system that produces undesirable management results. Most managers want to do a better job, and a new system is needed to help them do it.

Purpose of the Book

While there are many good ideas for managing more effectively, few comprehensive, integrated management systems are available. *Adding Value* offers such a system, which comprises three models: A, B, and C. The models are tools that individual managers can use to identify, organize, and capitalize on the best ideas emerging from the current business and organizational potential movement. Even more important, they offer a blueprint or a starter system for a shared-models approach to management and management development.

The management system proposed in *Adding Value* is unique in that it starts with the comprehensive needs of the business and from that derives the people, the skills, and the managerial roles required to fulfill those needs. It offers not just theoretical constructs but models that readers can use as hands-on tools. The system is also unique in that it distinguishes between the principles of management according to a business's needs and the ever-changing formulas that managers must continually create and revise to adapt the principles to the specific needs of the business. Finally, it is unique in that it factors shadow side realities into the day-to-day running of the company or institution.

(A brief aside: I use the phrase *companies and institutions* frequently because the framework and models outlined here apply to both for-profit and not-for-profit enterprises. Simply using the term *company* leaves the latter out. Moreover, I do not

use the term *organization* to mean company or institution. As
I indicate in my discussion of Model A, there is within any enterprise a difference between its *business*—its mandate, what it
is about, its strategic thrust—and its *organization*—the way it
structures itself and deploys its human resources to serve the
business. Therefore, with a few exceptions, I use the term *organization* in this more restricted sense.)

Overview of the Contents

Adding Value presents a management system that can help any
manager achieve better results. It examines three models based
on the needs of the business and briefly illustrates each model.
The first, Model A, spells out the needs of the business in terms
of strategy, operations, structure, human resource management
systems, management/supervision, and leadership. Model B specifies the needs of the business in terms of innovation and change
and outlines a shared process for instituting and managing
change. Model C presents an overview of the "shadow side" of
Models A and B, outlining the key "arational" factors involved
in designing, running, evaluating, and changing a business.
Model C also suggests ways in which the shadow side of the
system, for instance, the organizational culture, can be managed.
These three shared models constitute the management system.

The basic argument for a shared models approach is outlined in Chapter One. Chapter Two provides an overview of
Model A and its master tasks. Chapter Three discusses the
business dimensions of Model A, that is, strategy and operations. Chapter Four explores the organizational dimensions
of Model A, that is, structure and human resource management
systems, and presents the argument that the organization should
serve the business. Chapter Five deals with the management
and leadership dimensions of Model A, outlining the systematic
approaches needed to develop effective management and supervision and systemwide leadership. Chapter Six, which looks
retrospectively at Model A and prospectively at Model B, presents an overview of the shadow side realities that permeate
running and changing a business, together with some initial suggestions on how to manage these realities. All companies and

institutions need to change with the changing times; Chapter Seven provides an overview of a shared model for initiating and managing change, along with some suggestions on managing the shadow side of change. Managing the organizational culture is part of the role of the manager, and Chapter Eight recommends the learning organization paradigm, which emphasizes continual and pervasive improvement, as part of the preferred culture of any company or institution. Finally, Chapter Nine suggests ways that any company or institution can begin to develop such a comprehensive and integrated management system for itself.

Audience

Adding Value is addressed first of all to individual managers, who can take some of the ideas presented here and run with them without asking anyone's permission. They can also use the argument of the book to lobby for a more effective management system. Second, it is addressed to higher-level managers whose responsibility it is to create a management system that serves the business and provides a competitive edge. Third, management development and training specialists, whether internal or external, can use the system presented in the book to organize entire management development programs and tailor individual offerings to managers. Fourth, the system can be used by general management consultants as a blueprint for their businesses. For instance, consultants can use Model A as a tool for helping managers "take the pulse" of the company or institution and can use Model B to help companies institute and manage change. Fifth, the argument outlined is meant to challenge business schools in both their undergraduate and graduate programs; the system presented has implications for curriculum reform and development. Sixth, authors and publishers of management books, journals, and magazines may find in the system ways of organizing and even marketing their materials.

In addition, I believe that *Adding Value* would be especially useful for practitioners in the helping professions — counselors, nurses, psychologists, and social workers — who are interested either in making consulting a part of their practice or in moving into consulting entirely. Since I started in clinical psychology, the latter route is the one I have taken myself. Once I discovered that the social settings of people's lives contribute largely to their psychological problems, I became more interested in and engaged with communities, companies, and institutions. Thus the book is a good starting point for such professionals. It provides the big picture — the models, methods, and skills — that potential consultants need to get started. Model B, in particular, is the organizational adaptation of a helping model found in *The Skilled Helper* (Egan, 1990), a book many helping professionals have already used. Furthermore, since practitioners in the helping professions are accustomed to dealing with the "shadow side" of individuals, the transition to working with the shadow side of organizations should come to these professionals quite naturally.

There are potentially even more extensive societal benefits. *Adding Value* is meant to spark a debate that could lead to a dramatic increase in productivity both in for-profit and not-for-profit institutions. If poor management is one of the principal blocks to productivity and if comprehensive and integrated management systems tailored to the needs of each business or institution help increase the productivity of managers, the payoff from implementing such systems would be substantive increases in material wealth and human capital.

A Caveat

As a consultant, I work with companies and institutions on the assumption that the wisdom for improving every dimension of their management system lies within that organization. My job is to help them discover and mine that wisdom. The goal, then, is not so much about empowering people as it is about helping them use the power they already have; it is about removing the blocks to the use of this power. Similarly, all those who have a stake in more effective management already have the power they need to establish more effective management systems; they only need to debate what is needed and collaborate in its development. *Adding Value* is not meant to provide a definitive answer, but to stimulate debate about what an effective management system should involve.

The framework and the models within it are open-system models that need to be challenged, complemented, changed, refined, and developed if they are to meet the changing needs of companies and institutions. They need to be open to the best of business school research and to the business-improving ideas that are found on the shop floor. The "open architecture" approach taken in *Adding Value* encourages both the search for better ideas and the refinement of the ideas discovered.

Many examples are used in *Adding Value*. Examples are useful in illustrating points, but they do not in and of themselves prove anything. Examples are ways of showing what an idea looks like in practice or what worked in a particular company or institution. They are not meant to offer guarantees of any kind. Furthermore, giving examples of useful practice is not the same as identifying exemplars, that is, companies in a particular industry or institutions with a particular focus that do their work exceedingly well. It is not that identifying exemplars cannot be useful. Indeed, one of my standard questions as a consultant is, "Who in your industry does it best?" Quite often the managers with whom I am working answer, a bit weakly, "That's a good question." The problem with exemplars, as recent history demonstrates, is that they can fall from grace. That problem, as we shall see, tells us something about the nature of business and organizational excellence and its pursuit.

Acknowledgments

I am grateful to all the clients who have allowed me to explore and test with them many of the ideas I have presented. Many managers have had the courage to share with me not only their successes but also their doubts and failures. I have learned a great deal from both. Managers get bashed around quite a bit — by their direct reports, their peers, their bosses, the business press, and even themselves. I hope that *Adding Value* will help end the bashing and usher in a new era of managing and leading.

Chicago, Illinois GERARD EGAN
February 1993

The Author

G ERARD EGAN is professor of organization studies and psychology and program director for the Center for Organization Development (CORD) at Loyola University of Chicago. He received his B.A. degree (1953) in classics, his M.A. degree (1963) in philosophy, and his Ph.D. degree (1969) in clinical psychology, all from Loyola University.

Egan currently writes and conducts workshops and seminars, both in the United States and abroad, in the areas of business and organizational effectiveness, management development, leadership, the management of innovation and change, organizational politics and culture (the "shadow side" of the organization), communication, coaching, and counseling. He consults to a variety of companies and institutions worldwide. Clients he has worked with extensively include Amoco Corporation, British Airways, and the World Bank. He specializes in working with chief executives and senior managers, usually on a long-term basis, in strategy, business and organizational effectiveness, management and management development, leadership, the design and management of change, and organizational culture assessment and change.

In 1989 Egan received the University Associates Award

for Outstanding Contribution to the Field of Human Resource Development. Egan's books include *Interpersonal Living* (1976), *Change Agent Skills A: Assessing and Designing Excellence* (1988), *Change Agent Skills B: Managing Innovation and Change* (1988), and *The Skilled Helper* (fourth edition, 1990; Chinese, Dutch, French, German, Japanese, and Spanish translations).

Adding Value

ONE

The Foundations of Effective Management: A Systems Perspective

Picture the following scene: You drive up to a bridge in an unfamiliar area of the country. You have some concerns about how safe the bridge may be. There is a man standing next to the bridge, so you roll down the window and ask him his opinion. He says that he will give you the data and let you decide for yourself. He goes on to say, "This bridge was designed, engineered, constructed, and is currently being maintained by an engineering, construction, and maintenance firm all of whose professionals have been educated, selected, trained, and developed in the same way as the average manager is."

Would you cross that bridge? One manager said, "I shouldn't even be this close to it."

An Advanced Organizer: What Chapter One Is About

- *The Crisis in Management.* Numerous studies show that many managers do not manage well. This results from the way managers are chosen, trained, and supervised.
- *Crisis as Opportunity.* The flip side of managerial problems is managerial potential and opportunity.
- *Creating Value-Added Management.* The role of institutions is to create wealth, while the role of the manager is to add value.

Shared models of management can play an important part
in this process.

- *Overview of Models A, B, and C: The ABCs of Management.* Model
  A is a model of design, facilitation, and assessment; Model
  B deals with change; Model C is about managing the shadow
  side of the organization.
- *Managerial Competence.* Competence comes from meeting the
  needs of the business first. Managers need the kinds of skills
  that will help them meet these needs.
- *The Power of Shared Models.* Since they spell out the needs of
  the business, shared models (such as total quality management models) help managers take a systemic perspective,
  manage day-to-day messiness, and move beyond technical
  to managerial competence.

The Crisis in Management

While there are good, bad, and indifferent managers — as there
are good, bad, and indifferent members of other professions —
blaming managers for poor management is, to a large extent,
an instance of blaming the victim. Indeed, many, if not most,
managers tend to be victims of a poorly thought out and executed management system.

Three factors contribute greatly to the ineffectiveness of
many managers: the way they are chosen, the way they are
trained and developed, and the way they themselves are managed.

The Way Managers Are Chosen

Fred Simmons (not his real name) went to work as a scientist
fifteen years ago for a prestigious international agricultural research organization, one among a loosely related group of international agricultural research organizations influential in
promoting the green revolution in developing countries. He was
committed to doing the kind of strategic and applied research
that would benefit the hungry and malnourished in developing
countries. As he moved up in the organization, he acquired relatively light supervisory and managerial responsibilities. Management was not his forte, but he did the best he could.

A few years ago, however, these international agricultural research centers were asked by their donors to do more with less. The funding priorities of donor nations and development agencies were changing. While most donors agreed that the institutions were good at science, not all believed that they were as good as they could be at the effective and efficient delivery of strategic applied research. Therefore, donors and other stakeholders put a great deal of pressure on the research centers to manage themselves better. "Better management" meant formulating strategy that served the needs of clients more effectively, using strategy as a guide for doing research, designing organizations to support the strategy, including developing better interdepartmental collaboration and downsizing to a "mean and lean" state, and adopting the kind of performance management system that would help make all this happen. Therefore, senior scientists, including Fred Simmons, were asked to take on more managerial responsibilities.

This case highlights the way managers are often chosen. They are asked to manage not because they are seen as good managerial candidates capable of managerial work as such but because they are good at something else. Certified public accountants are asked to manage because they are skillful at auditing, engineers are asked to manage because they design bridges well, nurses who become head nurses are asked to manage and supervise because they know how to deliver health care. Good accountants, engineers, and nurses, however, do not necessarily make good managers. A good counselor or therapist will not necessarily run a mental health clinic well. Sometimes institutions do not even realize that they are asking people to assume managerial positions. For instance, priests are asked to run parishes and manage budgets without ever being prepared to do so. They are not chosen because they are good at managing; rather, they are promoted to managerial positions as a matter of course. In their new role, they are expected to add value in ways that are not clear to them. Managers in general are not chosen because of their supervisory and managerial potential. Rather, they are "ordained" as managers.

When individuals are chosen to be managers because they

are good at something else — engineering, accounting, marketing, sales, or whatever — they have a tendency to continue to do what they were good at before they became managers. They try to balance technical and managerial activities, often seeing the latter as a burden if not an outright waste of time. Since good sales representatives are chosen to be sales managers, in their new positions they often continue selling and thus fail to develop a sales strategy and an approach to the development of the sales force. Some newly promoted sales managers even end up interfering with the effectiveness of sales personnel. They are promoted to add value and instead they subtract value. When scientists in international agricultural research organizations end up in managerial positions, they often have difficulty balancing their own research with the quality of the research of those they manage. The latter can be as exciting as the former and add even greater value. But scientists are asked to be managers without understanding the scientific advantages of their new role. In general, individuals promoted to managerial positions do not always understand clearly their role as manager and the ways in which they can add value as a manager. And even if they do understand and appreciate the role, they may not possess the skills to implement it.

The Way Managers Are Trained and Developed

To paraphrase Robert Louis Stevenson, management is the only profession for which no preparation is thought necessary. Studies show that few managers, once chosen, receive systematic training in effective management. Once "ordained," new managers pick up whatever managerial skills they can along the way. It is true that most companies and institutions have some fund of managerial experience, intelligence, and wisdom into which new managers are socialized. They watch other managers, they receive coaching and mentoring, they read, they grab a seminar here and there, and, of course, they use their wits. However, this means that management development and training is often a hit-and-miss affair, something left to chance. A manager in one large, sophisticated company said, "When I promote someone to a managerial position, the first thing I do is send the person off on a two-week supervisory skills program. At least this gives them something." At the time, sending someone to a supervisory training program was considered enlightened practice in the company. Now, a few years later, the company, preparing to move aggressively into the twenty-first century, has opened a large management development and training center. But even though the bricks and mortar are in place, the success of the training center will depend on the quality of the management development programs and their integration into the business.

In the case of the international agricultural centers mentioned earlier, since some of the scientists were poor managers and supervisors, and others did not understand the role of manager in a research institution, management training and development programs were mounted. However, since many of the scientists did not join these centers in order to become managers, they found this new world of management both difficult and distasteful. Indeed, many who could not make the grade or refused to do so either left of their own accord or were asked to leave.

The Way Managers Are Managed

Not only are many managers thrown into their positions without managerial qualifications and then left untrained and undeveloped, but the very roles they assume are often unclear. As intelligent as they may be, they often are not sure how to add value to the enterprise. Furthermore, their managers — themselves victims of the system — often do little to help them. The average manager never gets a realistic, rounded picture of how to manage in the first place, and then, to add insult to injury, gets little or no guidance and feedback from his or her boss. It is almost assumed that managers do not need that kind of attention because they are managers. One company became almost infamous in its industry by choosing quality people for managerial positions and then daring them to succeed. The senior managers of this company, realizing their mistake, now sit in council when they are about to hire a manager for a key

RECRUITING/INTERVIEWING PROCESS

position and ask, What can we do to ensure that this new manager is a success?

These systemic failures are unfair both to managers at all levels and to the institutions within which they work. No one knows the productivity costs of poorly chosen, poorly trained, and poorly supervised managers. This state of affairs has gone unnoticed for a number of reasons.

- First, new managers tend to say nothing. For the neophyte to complain about his or her lack of preparation would mean risking the opportunity to climb the ladder.
- Second, many poor managers think they are doing well because they imitate what they saw their own managers doing. They have no other standards against which to rate themselves and get little or no feedback from others.
- Third, no one within any given company is calling attention to the disgraceful way that managers are chosen, trained, and developed.
- Fourth, the company's competitors are in the same boat; therefore, no one is calling attention to the competitive benefits of taking management and supervision seriously. Since competitors are choosing and developing managers in the same hit-and-miss way, managerial effectiveness is not immediately perceived as a competitive tool.
- Finally, the rush of everyday work distracts everyone from thinking too deeply about these issues.

In sum, no one notices how ineffective the managerial system is.

Crisis as Opportunity

Of course, the upside of all this is that the potential for improving both the managerial system and the effectiveness of individual managers is great in most companies and institutions. Indeed, it might be a relatively simple task to improve the performance of managers if the levers for improvement are both understood and used. One way of turning the crisis in management into opportunity is to turn the institutional and managerial deficits mentioned earlier into the development needs of managers. For instance, a review of common managerial failures provides the following set of guidelines:

- Choose managers with a capacity to become self-starting, self-directing, and autonomous.
- Make sure that managers really know what their job entails.
- Choose managers who actively seek value-added information (information, for instance, that calls for reformulating the company's strategy).
- Make it as easy as possible for managers to get value-added information.
- Help managers set business-enhancing goals and then discuss with them the paths to these goals together with the resources needed.
- Help managers engage in activities such as meetings, interactions with direct reports, and paperwork, that add value to the business.
- Give managers ongoing guidance and feedback on their performance.
- Establish a culture in which managers collaborate with one another.
- Help managers develop a managerial style that adds value to the business and facilitates the work of others.
- Take an active role in the development of managers as managers.

In sum, provide focus, support, and development for the institution's managers.

Another approach to improving the managerial system is to review the reasons businesses fail. What kinds of things can businesses do to thrive? Here is one checklist derived from a review of the factors contributing to the failure of a business:

- Make sure your managers know how to manage.
- Set strategy; keep it evergreen (responsive to changes in the business environment).
- Stay abreast of changes in the marketplace.

- Make sure that your managers have access to the information they need to make decisions.
- Control your inventory: balance cost against customer responsiveness.
- Make sure that the level of debt serves the business.
- Since cash is king, manage it well.
- Keep your banks informed.
- Keep your eye on costs.

It may be evident that this list was drawn up by a group of accountants.

Another way to improve the management system is to review the reasons businesses fail to become superior competitors. Pearson (1992), the former president of PepsiCo, outlined the "seven deadly sins" that U.S. businesses have been guilty of: (1) inconsistent product quality, (2) slow response to the marketplace, (3) lack of innovative, competitive products, (4) uncompetitive cost structure, (5) inadequate employee involvement, (6) unresponsive customer service, and (7) inefficient resource allocation. He also outlined what companies and institutions need to do in order to deal with these sins. Managers must know what the company or institution stands for, set and enforce higher and higher performance standards, institutionalize constant innovation, get involved in the substance of the business and not just administrative processes, recruit and develop the right kind of talent for a new kind of company, and create a system that emphasizes and rewards performance.

It is clear that there could be dozens of such lists, each with its own degree of helpfulness. But becoming bogged down in endless lists is a problem in itself. Rather, any company or institution can profit from a comprehensive and integrated business-effectiveness framework that enables it to establish and continually fine-tune its own list. To create such a list, however, it is essential to understand the needs of the business and how managers add value by meeting those needs.

Creating Value-Added Management

It is much more energizing to talk about the challenge of value-added management than to agonize over the problems of the management system and the failures of individual managers. The elements that must be considered in meeting this challenge include the following:

- The overall purpose of the company or institution — to create wealth
- The basic role of the manager — to add value
- The role of shared models of management
- The design, facilitation, and assessment of the company or institution (Model A)
- Initiation and management of change (Model B)
- Management of the shadow side of the organization (Model C)

Each of these points is discussed in turn in the following sections.

The Purpose of the Institution: Creating Wealth

Well-run businesses and institutions create wealth for the society in which they operate. While for-profit businesses create material wealth, not-for-profit and human service institutions create human capital or wealth. Counseling the troubled and helping them manage problems in living more effectively, creating learning opportunities for young and old alike, helping children grow and develop, healing the sick, providing stability and a sense of belonging through the formation of religious community — all these activities create human capital, human wealth. Furthermore, since the best for-profit companies tend to develop or leverage their human assets in the pursuit of financial goals, they benefit society by creating both material and human wealth.

    Managers, then, play a critical role in creating wealth. Managers in pharmaceutical companies contribute in a wide variety of ways to the steady flow of products that meet the needs of their ultimate customers. Managers in agricultural research centers contribute to the steady flow of strategic and applied research that benefits people in developing countries. Administrators in educational institutions contribute to the creation of human capital and wealth through the learning, growth, and development of students.

The Role of the Manager: Adding Value

If the basic purpose of the company or institution is to create
wealth, then the primary role of the manager is to add value
to this wealth-creating process. One manager may add value
by reconceptualizing and refocusing a part of the company's
strategy, another by finding a more effective way of marketing
a product, a third by playing a role in the redesign of a manufacturing process, a fourth by developing and implementing a more
effective approach to customer service, a fifth by making sure
that everyone understands how a new structure will serve the
business and what needs to be done to make the new structure
work, a sixth by choosing and developing the best people for
a new project, and so forth. The ideal, of course, is that each
manager add value through each activity in which he or she
engages every day. Effective managers do not call or participate in meetings that add no value to the business. They try
to add value through every conversation they have. Effective
managers add value to their enterprises through their day-to-
day decisions and activities. Ineffective managers add cost rather
than value. Effective managers make value-added things happen, often through others. Managers are usually not neutral.
They add either net value or cost.

The Role of Shared Models of Management

The trick, of course, is to know what to do to add value, which
is the basic premise of this book:

      1.   Managers would manage more effectively and add
greater value to their companies and institutions if, like other
professionals, they trained in and worked from comprehensive,
integrated models of effective management.
      2.   The models should be derived from the needs of the
business and be shared by all managers.
      3.   The models should serve as the basis for management
selection, training, and development.

Most professionals such as doctors and engineers work from shared models, principles, methods, and skills. Establishing integrated and comprehensive models for understanding and dealing with the requirements of a business constitutes a major step toward clarifying and professionalizing the role of manager. Shared models of management contribute to the kind of alignment of managerial resources that serves the purpose of a company or institution and keeps it on course. They help managers know how to add value to the enterprise.

Overview of Models A, B, and C: The ABCs of Management

Adding Value proposes three shared models of management, called Models A, B, and C — the ABCs of value-added management. Figure 1.1 displays the relationship between the three models.

Model A: Managing Business and Organizational Processes

The most comprehensive of the three models of value-added management proposed in this book, Model A deals with business, organizational, managerial, and leadership effectiveness. It focuses on strategy, operations, organizational and job structure, human resource management systems, general management systems, and leadership. Model A provides answers to three basic questions:

1. *Design*. How do we design or redesign a company or any part of it, integrating business, organizational, and managerial factors?
2. *Facilitation*. Once the unit is up and running, how do we make it work day in and day out?
3. *Assessment*. How do we determine how well the business is working?

Model A is not a theory. It is a pragmatic process managers can use to review the needs of the business and those of the organization that is to serve the business. Model A can be used

Figure 1.1. The ABC Triangle: The Interactive Nature of Models A, B, and C.

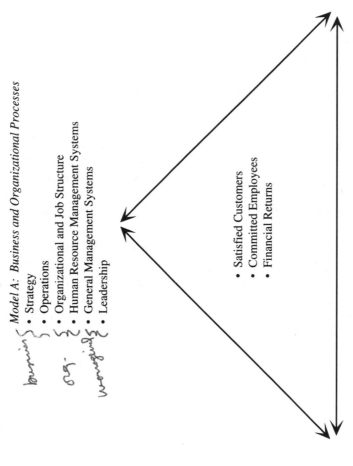

Model A: Business and Organizational Processes
- Strategy
- Operations
- Organizational and Job Structure
- Human Resource Management Systems
- General Management Systems
- Leadership

- Satisfied Customers
- Committed Employees
- Financial Returns

Model B: Change
- Environmental Change
- Remedial Change
- Innovative Change
- Continual Improvement

Model C: Shadow Side of the Organization
- Business and Organizational Messiness
- Employee Idiosyncrasies
- The Social System
- Organizational Politics
- Organizational Culture

to design, manage, or assess an entire corporation, company, or institution, any of its subunits, or any function, project, or program. It is a comprehensive and integrated map of the tasks that need to be done to make the business work, to make the organization serve the business effectively, and to develop a cadre of managers and leaders to coordinate and facilitate the execution of business and organizational processes.

def.

Model A is the most important of the three models because it answers the question, What do we need to do to produce satisfied customers, committed employees, and good financial returns (or, in the case of not-for-profit institutions, "value for money")? Chapters Two, Three, and Four provide a discussion of Model A.

Model B: Initiating and Managing Change

Model B provides a comprehensive framework for instituting and managing innovation and change (see Egan, 1988). Relevant questions are, What do we need to do to make the business better? How can we make the organization serve the business more effectively? How do we improve management and leadership around here? If, as the saying goes, change has become the only constant in companies and institutions, then having a common model for initiating and managing change is a basic requirement for both institutional and managerial effectiveness. A versatile and flexible model of change is needed, one that can be used for instituting and managing change, managing the fallout from change, coping with the impact of external change, and tackling day-to-day problem solving and opportunity development. Model B, which is discussed in Chapter Seven, meets all these demands.

Model C: Managing the Shadow Side of the Organization

Model C specifies a framework for helping managers and other agents of change deal with aspects of the system that are other than rational. Managers spend a great deal of time managing the nonsense of the system. Managing the "shadow side" of the institution includes the following:

- Managing day-to-day business and organizational messiness
- Coping with the idiosyncracies and problems of employees
- Meeting the challenges of the organization as a social system
- Dealing with the ups and downs of organizational politics
- Managing the positive and negative dimensions of organizational culture

The organizational culture has been called "the largest and most controlling aspect of the system" because it dictates the norms according to which everything, including the elements of the other four shadow side categories, is run. Since culture and other shadow side realities permeate every facet of Models A and B, the ability to understand and manage these realities is central to the role of general manager. Managing the shadow side is explored in Chapter Six.

Models A, B, and C are templates to help managers discover the needs of the business. These models are continuously open to challenge, revision, and improvement. They must be our tools, not our masters.

Managerial Competence

Helping managers consistently add more value to the business is the fundamental goal of value-added management, but finding ways to do that has proved difficult. What may be needed is a shift in perspective — from one focusing on the needs of the manager to one concentrating on the needs of the business.

The Traditional Approach: Process Skills

In general, texts on management have focused on the skills of the manager. Many texts organize managerial skills around the major managerial activities of planning, organizing, staffing, directing, controlling, and leading. In recent years, a number of management texts, taking a more personal turn, have emphasized both the management of self and the supervision of others — management with a more human face, as it were. These texts include such skills as developing self-awareness, managing personal stress, solving problems creatively, establishing supportive communication, gaining power and influence, improving employee performance through motivation, empowering employees, delegating and decision making, managing conflict, conducting effective group meetings, and team building. The emphasis in these more personal skills, however, is still the manager and his or her activities. This can be called a *process approach* to managerial competence.

A Content Approach:
Emphasizing the Needs of the Business

In the give-and-take of everyday business a more pragmatic approach to managerial competence is needed. The perspective is different. In day-to-day operations the principal managerial questions are, What should I work on? What outcomes will best serve the business? It may mean putting the finishing touches on a new strategy, translating the company's grand strategy into a strategy for a particular functional unit, getting the product mix right, putting into place a more effective and efficient work program, hiring the right person, redesigning a job, dividing up the work in a more equitable way, helping an employee redirect his or her energies, or making sure that everyone in the unit understands which values are to drive the business. The list is endless, but business-serving outcomes is the focus.

Content skills are derived from the needs of the business itself and from organizational realities insofar as they serve the business. These include such things as the ability to

- Formulate, implement, and fine-tune strategy
- Stay in touch with the changing needs of customers
- Design effective and efficient work programs
- Make sure that business-enhancing quality and customer service programs are in place
- Establish cost-containment procedures
- Formulate and reformulate the structure to make sure that it continues to serve the business
- Find new ways of making a reasonable structure work

- Establish jobs and roles with the kind of flexibility that serves the business
- Help design the kind of human resource management systems that help workers give their best efforts
- Find ways of making sure that well-designed human resource systems are effectively used by managers and supervisors
- Choose managers and supervisors mainly because of their managerial and supervisory potential
- Help establish a management development process and make it work
- Develop and use the performance management system as a tool for increased productivity
- Develop strategic, operational, and human resource plans to make sure that all the above happens
- Move institution-enhancing agendas through changing political currents within the organization
- Create and reinforce the kind of culture that serves the business
- Exercise leadership to achieve results beyond the ordinary, in all the above

These are the areas in which managers need to deliver business-enhancing outcomes. To be sure, planning, organizing, staffing, directing, controlling, leading, and the other process skills go into accomplishing these objectives, but content skills are primary.

The Power of Shared Models

There are many advantages of working from shared models of managing: shared models enable managers to take a systemic approach to management, they help bring order to the chaos of day-to-day managerial activities, and they help distinguish between managerial and technical activities.

A Systemic Approach to Management

The power of shared management models is dramatically illustrated in many companies and institutions that have successfully adopted quality as a strategic driver. Quality in and of itself is not a management program; it is an aspect of a product or service. In its wider sense, however, as in total quality management (TQM) programs, quality encompasses everything in the company or institution: strategy, customers' requirements, work design and flow, products and services, customer service, organizational structure, human resource management systems, coaching and counseling, systemwide leadership, and so on. While many companies have approached TQM in a halfhearted way, others have pursued it with a vigor that has yielded excellent results.

The difference in results probably does not come primarily from quality itself, though quality is not to be underestimated. Rather, those businesses that have achieved excellent results have done so because, for the first time, all managers within the institution have a shared systemic model of management, a template for doing things properly, a comprehensive process together with a common language. Such quality professionals as Deming, Juran, and Crosby give managers not a hodgepodge of dictums about quality but an integrated system of managing. Deming's approach focuses more on the company itself, rather than individual managers. He has claimed that when it comes to poor quality, the system, not individuals, is the problem in 85 percent of the cases. Therefore, it is impossible to improve quality without managers' having a comprehensive quality framework together with the methods and skills to understand and improve every dimension of the system itself.

Quality is not the only basis for a comprehensive and integrated system of managing. Some companies use marketing to achieve the same goal. They cry that "the business is all about marketing." In such cases the full marketing system is a shared framework for managing that provides focus, direction, and a language for talking about every aspect of the business.

Since Models A, B, and C are systemic models, they provide comprehensive templates for action. They constitute the "total" part of TQM.

Putting Order into Day-to-Day Managerial Activities

Most managers know from experience that any given day may be a hectic mishmash of attending to a range of demands and interactions, many of them unplanned. The Pareto Principle is a principle of leverage. Applied to management, it suggests that managers get about 80 percent of their results from about 20 percent of their activities.

Since managers are continually deciding what to pay attention to and what to use their time on, they can benefit from broad but pragmatic frameworks or models that help them understand and choose what is important. Shared models form the basis of pragmatic "menus" managers can use to choose value-added activities and interventions. Models A, B, and C provide the principles and guidelines for both keeping the enterprise on track and improving it.

Distinguishing Managerial from Technical Skills

Since managers are chosen to manage because they have proved themselves to be competent at something else, they usually take on the managerial role equipped with a solid set of technical skills, for instance, engineering, finance, marketing, human resource, R&D, or manufacturing skills. The initial temptation for new managers is to continue to do what they did before; as pointed out earlier, they often see the new managerial demands as an obstacle to be overcome. Furthermore, technical skills, especially skills in finance and accounting, can masquerade for managerial skills. In some cases managers believe that since finance and accounting are primary business skills, they are also the primary managerial skills. In some companies engineers are made senior managers because engineering is at the heart of the business. However, while an engineering background can help the manager understand the business, engineering skills are not managerial skills.

Technical skills take precedence over managerial skills in other ways. In many business schools, managers specialize in marketing, information systems, finance, accounting, manufacturing, operations, and other facets of the business. As business schools add curriculum niches in order to survive, there is a tendency to increase the number of these specialties — retail management, health care management, real estate management, and the like. There is no doubt that the skills needed for these specialties are useful, but it is doubtful that one can become a good manager simply by learning these specialties.

Of course, companies and institutions could hire people with such specialties — accountants, manufacturing experts, finance experts, and so forth — but use their skills without making them managers. Their work could then be coordinated by managers with expertise in management itself. Managers, at least ideally, have a perspective much broader than any of these specialties. If these experts are made managers in their own specialties, however, companies should first make sure that they develop an institution-enhancing range of management skills. Developing expertise in management should be a prerequisite for promotion to higher managerial positions.

It has been demonstrated over and over again that companies in trouble have been saved by managers who have financial and accounting skills. It has also been demonstrated that some companies have done better when managers with technical skills have replaced managers with just financial skills or general managers. Some of the best companies in the world, however, are run by skilled general managers.

A general manager, in the sense used here, is a manager at any level who understands the context in which the institution or unit within the institution functions and who knows what it needs to survive and thrive. General managers know how to orchestrate diverse functions and stakeholders in the service of the whole. Hospital administrators need not be doctors, but they do need to understand the health care industry and the diverse functions and needs of their particular health care facility. High school principals need not be specialists in any given discipline, nor need they be teachers, but they do need to know what is going on in secondary education and to orchestrate the diverse departments and resources of the school to serve the learning, growth, and development of students.

Models A, B, and C provide templates that general managers can use to orchestrate the diverse functions of the institution or of the unit to fulfill its mission and to initiate change.

The kind of manager — generalist, technical specialist,

business specialist, or whatever—that any institution needs at a given time depends on circumstances. Technical managers of whatever stripe, however, will do better if they complement their technical skills with a solid set of general management skills to prevent their technical expertise from becoming the tail that wags the dog.

A No-Formula Approach to Value-Added Management

We live in the day of the quick fix. Managers are bombarded by brochures that promise quick fixes for everything. Models A, B, and C, on the other hand, provide the principles and areas required for effective managerial activities. They do not provide ready-made formulas. It is the job of the manager to tailor these principles to the needs of the business. Each business needs to develop its own formulas.

Taking management seriously, then, means developing a cadre of managers who have the working knowledge, skills, and commitment—as managers rather than technicians—to make the business work, to make the organization serve the business, to continually improve both, and to enlist the efforts of everyone else in these endeavors. It helps to start with pragmatic, business-oriented models that help managers explore the needs of the business. What needs to be done to add value to the business? is question one. What skills do managers need to do it? is question two. The rest of the book answers these questions.

TWO

A Model for Business, Organizational, and Leadership Effectiveness

Model A, which provides an integrated picture of a well-run for-profit or not-for-profit enterprise, is the central model of this book. It has three major parts: business effectiveness, organizational effectiveness, and managerial and leadership effectiveness. This chapter provides an overview of the entire model. Chapter Three focuses on the business dimensions of the model, including strategy and operations. Chapter Four deals with the organizational dimensions of the model, including structure and human resources. Chapter Five discusses the managerial and leadership dimensions of the model.

An Advanced Organizer: What Chapter Two Is About

- *The Basic Requirements of an Enterprise.* A shared framework that outlines the needs of the company or institution helps managers add value.
- *The Necessity for Working Models.* Managers need practical tools to make the enterprise work.
- *Model A: Design, Facilitation, and Assessment.* Model A helps managers design, run, and "take the pulse" of the enterprise. The desired outcomes of the model are satisfied customers, a committed and productive workforce, and decent financial

results. Model A provides six master tasks that outline the needs of the enterprise and present ways to achieve the desired outcomes.

The Basic Requirements of an Enterprise

Jerry Porras (1987), a professor at Stanford University who has consulted with a variety of companies and institutions, made a case for a shared design, facilitation, and assessment framework (a Model A framework), and offered his own. He argues that leading, managing, and changing institutions is difficult enough, but is made even more difficult because managers do not have a clear-cut model of an effectively operating company or institution. It is essential to know what the components of a company or institution are, how they are put together, and how changing one (such as strategy) affects another (such as human resource planning).

Few managers use a comprehensive and integrated framework to guide their efforts. Many do have some kind of model, but it is often intuitive and idiosyncratic, one carried around inside their heads and not generally shared with others. Moreover, this "in the head" model is not comprehensive or integrated. For instance, it may focus on operations but ignore strategy. Or it may focus on strategy but ignore the managerial processes needed to get strategy to touch everything in the system. To make things worse, managers forget key parts of their working models in times of crisis. The lack of a comprehensive, integrating framework makes management and the management of change a much more erratic process than it need be. Moreover, the lack of a shared framework is one of the things that prevents the members of the system from pulling together as a team.

The Necessity for Working Models

Managers need working models rather than theoretical ones. A working model is an outline or visual portrayal of how things actually work. It is a kind of cognitive map that shows people how something is put together or illustrates the steps in a process, showing how one step follows from another. A working model is one that enables the user to achieve concrete and specific goals efficiently. Unassembled furniture, for instance, is accompanied by a set of illustrated instructions that show the buyer how to assemble it. The buyer, then, has a working model that enables him or her to perform a task. Working models differ from models that merely explain something conceptually. While purely conceptual models can ultimately be very useful, often they can be too abstract or too complicated to serve as frameworks for immediate action.

Two criteria characterize working models: (1) they must be complex enough to account for the reality they attempt to portray, and (2) they must be simple enough to use. A model that meets only the first criterion is likely to be of interest only to theoreticians and researchers. A model that meets only the second criterion would tend to be simplistic rather than merely simple and would be useless as a working model.

In summary, then, working models, as opposed to models devised primarily to explain systems, have the following advantages:

- They provide a means for translating theory and research into a visualization of how things work.
- They constitute a framework for action or intervention.
- They suggest the methods, technologies, and skills needed to get the work done.
- They are simple without being simplistic.

Working models such as TQM blueprints, customer service strategies, and business-focused performance management systems, when shared by the managers within an institution, can be powerful managerial tools.

Model A: Design, Facilitation, and Assessment

Model A is a working model — a design, facilitation, and assessment framework that is simple to use but still comprehensive enough to cover all key business, organizational, managerial, and leadership areas. As suggested in Chapter One, Model A can be used in three different ways. First, as a design model, it can be used to design the entire enterprise, any of the units within it, such as the human resources department, or any project or program. Second, as a facilitation model, it provides the overall principles managers need to help make the system work effectively. Third, as an assessment model, it can be used to assess or "take the pulse" of the entire system or any dimension of it.

Model A offers a general management perspective. While managers have their own departmental functions to look after, they must also wear a "general manager" hat to make sure that what they are doing contributes to the overall effectiveness of the company or institution. At times general manager considerations can clash with, say, manager-engineer considerations. Model A is a framework derived from and designed to promote the kind of "systems thinking" that is needed to keep a general management point of view front and center.

Three Desired Outcomes

Model A focuses on three major outcomes that all companies and institutions strive for: satisfied customers, committed and productive employees, and good financial returns (or in the case of not-for-profit institutions, good "value for money").

Satisfied Customers. Companies and institutions exist to serve the needs and wants of customers. Apparel store customers are satisfied when they get the goods they want in the right style and at the right price and with the right degree of customer service. Satisfied customers tend to return. In schools the customers are students. The school is successful when their needs to learn, grow, and develop are satisfied. A human resources department has internal customers. When the various departments of the company get the right people with the right skills and the right compensation package, they, too, are satisfied.

Committed and Productive Employees. The ideal is productive workplaces in which both productivity and the quality of work life is high. Over the years one U.S. enterprise, Lincoln Electric Company, has been singled out for living up to this ideal. In that company there is a "benign" rather than a vicious cycle in place — employees share in the company's success, which in turn spurs them to greater productivity, which keeps financial results high and leads to the next turn of the benign cycle.

Financial Returns. In Chapter One it was suggested that the overall goal of companies and institutions is the creation of wealth in terms of either material wealth or human capital. Not-for-profits do well when they achieve their goals efficiently, that is, they get value for money. For instance, many charities, in giving an account of themselves, take pride in low administrative costs. This means that more of the contributions received go directly into the charitable work of the institutions. In for-profit enterprises, while the overall goal is the creation of material wealth, profit itself, according to some, is not a goal but rather an indication of how well the entire enterprise is being managed. According to this line of thought, the cost-effective delivery of products and services to customers is the overriding goal.

Achieving the Desired Outcomes: The Six Master Tasks

What do managers need to do to get the desired mix of satisfied customers, committed and productive employees, and good financial returns? Model A provides six master tasks or pragmatic guiding principles for achieving this mix. They deal with (1) strategy, (2) operations, (3) structure, (4) human resources, (5) management and supervision, and (6) leadership. They are called "master tasks" because, first, they are the major tasks facing any company or institution in the pursuit of success, and second, each master task includes a number of subtasks. While every company engages in all of these master tasks, some are more important to one company than to another, and some are more important to the same company at one time of its existence than at another. For instance, while strategy may be more important for IBM than for a three-person management consulting firm, strategy still has some importance for the latter. And, while strategy was important but not critical for oil companies when the world economy was less turbulent, getting the strategy right has now moved to center stage.

Master Task One: Strategy. *Formulate a strategy that provides over-all focus and direction.* When Bernard Brennan, the current CEO and chair of Montgomery Ward, took over the helm, the first thing he did was to fashion a specialty retail strategy for the failing company. The retailer dumped the unprofitable catalogue business and focused on five businesses: Electric Avenue, Home Ideas, the Apparel Store, Gold'n Gems, and Auto Express. The strategy injected new life into the retailer and was one of the principal factors in the company's turnaround. Ideally, strategy puts its mark on everything that happens within a company or institution.

Master Task Two: Operations. *Deliver valued products and services cost-effectively to customers.* Operations translates strategy into customer-satisfying action. Detroit Diesel, by staying close to both employees and customers, improving quality, and constantly finding ways of working faster, moved from a 3.2 percent market share at the time of its buyout from General Motors to a 23 percent share in 1991. In a year that was a disaster for many retailers, The Gap added 123 new stores and significantly increased both revenues and profits by offering simple but eye-catching styles, quality goods, and reasonable prices. Many companies have been turning operational factors such as quality and customer service into "strategic drivers."

Master Task Three: Structure. *Design the kind of organizational structure needed to optimize information sharing, decision making, and work flow.* IBM has found its old, centralized structure too cumbersome for the new fast-moving competitive environment of the computer industry. The company, struggling to decentralize, announced in the latter part of 1992 its plans to form a subsidiary to develop, manufacture, and sell its personal computers. In an era in which speed to market is essential, many companies have established teams and redesigned jobs to provide much greater workplace flexibility. One General Electric plant adopted a team system that allowed it to change product models a dozen times a day. The result was a 250 percent increase in productivity.

Master Task Four: Human Resource Management Systems. Develop human resource management systems that managers and supervisors can use to help workers give their best. Leveraging the human assets of an enterprise is just as important as leveraging its financial assets. Federal Express won an award for effective human resource management by effectively training all its employees in the basics of service delivery and by keeping them attuned to its wide array of business-enhancing changes — over fifteen hundred in 1991 — through ongoing information sharing and training efforts. An employee action team found a way of reducing the time needed for one critical training program from six to three weeks. Levi Strauss and Company won an award for developing a human resources function that has helped develop a working partnership between the company and its employees. Now everyone is committed to finding practical ways to accomplish three basic goals: to implement the company's mission, vision, and values; to continually improve everything the firm does; and to promote the health, safety, and well-being of all employees.

Master Task Five: Value-Added Management. Develop a cadre of skilled and enthusiastic managers and supervisors to play a critical role in accomplishing the six master tasks and to provide coordination, direction, and support for all workers. In the 1990s General Electric established a management system that focused on both productivity and an employee-involving management style. Managers who achieved results but violated the values of the supervisor-worker partnership were in jeopardy. In 1992 Amoco Chemical Company put in place a set of management principles involving strategic management, the delivery of quality processes, products, and services, the use of information, measurement, and analysis, the development and management of human resources, and the achievement of environmental, health, and safety goals.

Master Task Six: Pragmatic Leadership. Develop leaders at every level of the organization to provide institution-enhancing innovation and change. Since leadership can mean so many things, any company wanting to develop leaders must tell its people what it means by leadership and what kind or kinds of leadership would best serve the company's interest. All forms of leadership must be results oriented, the essence of leadership being the achievement of results beyond the ordinary. In 1990 and 1991 Ford sent some three thousand managers to a custom-designed eight-day program on leadership at the University of Michigan. In 1992 Montgomery Ward began a process of introducing all its managers to strategic leadership that involved producing results "beyond the ordinary" in three key areas: the cascading and implementation of strategy, the improvement of customer service, and the business-enhancing development of people.

In any given company or institution all six master tasks are in play at the same time and, ideally, integrated with one another. The strategy is continually being cascaded down through the system; products and services that translate the strategy are continually being designed, developed, and delivered; the structure is continually being fine-tuned to support the strategy and optimize work flow; managers and supervisors are continually using human resource management systems to help people give their best; managers as both managers of processes and supervisors of people are finding new ways of adding value to the business; and a corps of leaders are involved in continually improving every aspect of the business. This process is summarized in the simple "pursuit of excellence" task cycle outlined in Figure 2.1.

The six master tasks can be divided into three major divisions, which parallel the three governing principles of Model A: Tasks one and two deal with the business of the system; tasks three and four deal with the organization of the system; tasks five and six deal with the management and leadership dimensions of the system.

- First, get your business in shape, in terms of both strategy and operations.
- Second, fashion an organization, including structure and

Figure 2.1. Model A: The Pursuit of Excellence Task Cycle.

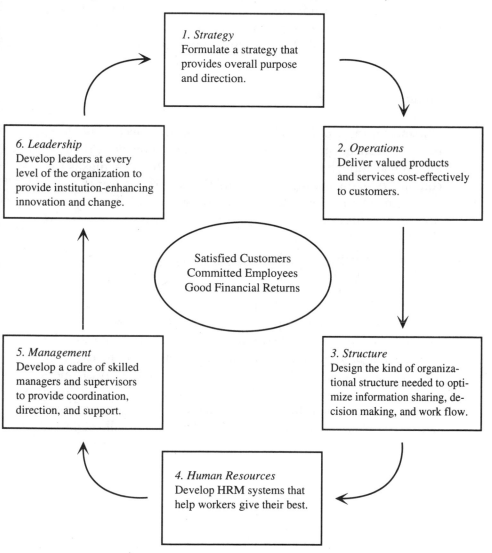

1. Strategy
Formulate a strategy that
provides overall purpose
and direction.

6. Leadership
Develop leaders at every
level of the organization to
provide institution-enhancing
innovation and change.

2. Operations
Deliver valued products
and services cost-effectively
to customers.

Satisfied Customers
Committed Employees
Good Financial Returns

5. Management
Develop a cadre of skilled
managers and supervisors
to provide coordination,
direction, and support.

3. Structure
Design the kind of organizational structure needed to optimize information sharing, decision making, and work flow.

4. Human Resources
Develop HRM systems that
help workers give their best.

human resource management systems, that serves your business rather than itself.

- Third, choose and develop the kind of managers and leaders
  needed to play critical roles in making the business work
  and the organization serve the business effectively.

These categories help focus a manager's attention. For instance, a company should not continue to pour money into a TQM program if its managers lack basic management skills; it should train them in such skills or recruit managers already possessing them.

Managing Complexity

The master tasks of Model A are the tasks that need to be done to create a successful enterprise. Please note, however, that the apparent simplicity of the master tasks of Model A masks the complexity of the manager's role and the day-to-day frenzy mentioned in Chaper One. Chapters Three through Five, which present the subtasks of each master task, show the reason for the frenzy.

Furthermore, Model A is depicted as a rational, systematic, and linear method for designing, facilitating, and "taking the pulse" of companies and institutions and the various units within them. It outlines the logic of business, organizational, managerial, and leadership effectiveness and provides systematic answers to commonly asked questions: What are the essential elements of any enterprise? How do the elements fit together and interact? What needs to be done to make an enterprise operate more effectively? As noted in Chapter One, however, logic and reason have their limits. There are shadow side factors that permeate all six master tasks of Model A, as we will see later.

THREE

The Requirements
of Business

The first part of Model A deals with strategy and operations, or the business dimensions of the company or institution. Note that the term *business* as I am using it does not refer to a for-profit enterprise. It refers to the strategy of any enterprise, for-profit or not-for-profit, and the way that strategy is translated into a set of operations through which products and services are delivered to customers. In this sense we can talk about the "business" of a church or a mental health clinic just as we can talk about the business of an airline or a computer firm. If church leaders are asked what business they are in, they might reply that they are in the business of saving souls or that they are in the business of helping people form communities centered around their religious beliefs and values.

An Advanced Organizer: What Chapter Three Is About

- *Master Task One: Strategy.* Formulate a strategy that provides overall focus and direction for the company or institution. The subtasks of strategy involve defining the mission and vision of an enterprise, setting its values, determining which products and services are to be offered to which markets, identifying the core competencies needed to produce and

deliver the products and services, and exploring the business environment in which the enterprise is to operate.
- *Master Task Two: Operations.* Translate strategy into a set of operations that deliver valued products and services to customers. The subtasks of operations include customer focus, the design of products and services, cost-effective work design and flow, quality assurance, research and development, marketing, customer service, the management of material resources, and the use and tracking of financial resources.

Master Task One: Strategy

Strategy is the first of the two business dimensions of Model A. The principle dealing with strategy is clear enough:

Master Task One: Formulate a strategy that provides overall focus and direction for the company or institution.

The term *strategy* is used in a variety of ways. It is often used, sometimes in the plural, to indicate ways of achieving goals and objectives; for example, "We want to reduce the size of our work force by 20 percent, and early retirement is one of the strategies we will use to achieve this goal." In this sense, *strategy* refers to a set of activities that will produce a desired result and achieve certain goals. With respect to Model A, however, we are talking about strategy in a larger sense, strategy that provides overall focus and direction for a business. This kind of strategy defines who we are, what we are about, where we are going, what drives us, what we have to offer, and what our major goals are.

The Pragmatic Nature of Strategy

When Bernard Brennan took over as CEO at Montgomery Ward, the company needed a whole raft of operational, structural, managerial, and cultural changes, but strategy was to be the principal tool for making all the other changes happen. Many managers were involved in hammering out the strategy, but the time was well spent. The turnaround in the fortunes of Montgomery Ward has been directly related to the formulation of a viable strategy. The challenge now is to make sure that strategy touches everything else in the company.

Many companies and institutions fail to develop a strategy, or they develop a strategy that is not viable, or they formulate a viable strategy and then fail to get it to drive the business, or they give up on a good strategy as soon as the first obstacle comes along. Some conglomerates are unwilling to forge strategy for the entire corporation. Their leaders claim that the corporate strategy is nothing more than a summation of all the strategies of the different businesses. However, even though these businesses have their own strategies, it is my experience that they still seek direction — which is not to be confused with interference — from the corporation itself.

Here is a case in point. I worked with one international development institution that had no strategy beyond its original charter. While many managers had a sense of mission and purpose, they did not have a sense of strategy. The CEO wondered why few strategic ideas seemed to well up from the ranks of middle management and why so much of the good work of the institution seemed to be diffused and without impact. The institution had an operational focus, which was the day-to-day delivery of needed and well-intentioned services. The lack of strategy, however, was a disservice to the dedicated people who had given their lives to this institution.

On the other hand, I have worked with other international development institutions — principally international agricultural research centers — that saw strategy as the foundation of their work. Their impact on the nutritional needs of developing countries has often been profound.

The Subtasks of Strategy

Managers add value by bringing a strategic perspective to everything they do in order to provide focus and direction for the entire system. There has been some criticism of the narrow approach some companies and institutions take to the formulation of strategy. For instance, so-called strategy is often restricted to statistical analysis, next year's strategy being merely an extrapolation from last year's numbers. In Model A, however, the subtasks of strategy deal with nine complex and interrelated elements, which are enumerated as follows:

1.   Mission. Who are we? What are we about? What business are we in? A company's mission clarifies its raison d'être, establishes its identity, and defines what business the company is in. An airline at one time considered getting into the integrated travel business — flight, rental cars, and hotels — but management decided that this was a case of wedding volatile businesses to volatile businesses. So the company decided to remain in the commercial airline business with a focus on both domestic and international travel. It entered into strategic alliances with travel companies and became the dominant airline with some, but decided to stay away from the package travel part of the business.

2.   Vision. What are our dreams and aspirations? Where do we want to go? What do we want to look like in five years? Vision adds some "soul" to the strategy, though it is also based on the rational premise that companies that set "stretch" goals do better than those that set either easily attainable or impossible goals. The airline mentioned earlier decided it wanted to become one of the major global players in the airline industry and to be considered as good as some of the best. The airline certainly wanted to be big; but their commitment to being both big and excellent in the eyes of their customers was not that clear. Industry analysts believed that the airline was very good at bread-and-butter tasks, but not at such things as providing the kind of service offered by airlines in the top tier.

3.   Values. What do we prize? What drives our business? What are our criteria for making business, organizational, managerial, leadership, and ethical decisions? While values such as bigness, aggressiveness, and boldness drove the airline's business, the company came up much shorter on people-related values. Customer service was paid lip service but was not yet a strategic driver. The company seemed to almost prefer an adversarial relationship with its own employees. It did prize safety and had one of the best records in the industry. The company needed to develop and communicate a much more coherent set of values, one that gave more credence to its vision.

4. Markets. Which markets should we be in? Which markets do we need to create? What should be our basic customer orientation in these markets? The airline developed four strong hubs with good geographic spread in the United States. Its strategy was to enter preferred markets by buying the routes and assets of troubled carriers. It bought the Asian routes of a weaker airline and then went on to do the same for European and South American routes. Finally, it targeted a couple of Europe-Asia routes so it could offer around-the-world service. The company also took significant stakes in a number of commuter or feeder airlines in order to serve small-town markets. In a word, this was a company with market savvy and muscle.

5. Core Competencies. What are we good at? What do we need to be good at? How can we leverage our competencies into products and services for the markets we serve? The airline was good at such things as financial management, logistics, information systems, fleet development, aircraft maintenance, and market development. It needed to develop competencies in marketing, catering, customer service, managing in different cultures, and, generally, dealing with people. Because of poor service it initially stumbled in the Asian market, where superb service offered unobtrusively and seamlessly was the order of the day.

6. Products and Services. What kinds of products or services should we provide for the markets we serve? How do we use these products to carve out a market niche? The airline focused a great deal of energy on business customers. It developed a special product for full-fare economy passengers that included special seating and preferred treatment at the time of reservations and at check-in. The company developed a frequent flyer program that appealed to business travelers and had a policy of "sweetening the pot" with a variety of incentives to keep even demanding customers on the tether.

7.   *Business Environment. What threats and opportunities do we face from such environmental factors as competition, the economy, the physical environment, industry trends, regulatory agencies, and foreign governments? How should we track key environmental activities and trends?* The airline believed that global competitors with financial muscle would survive. It believed that the wave of deregulation that had swept the United States would eventually sweep through Europe and even Asia. And so it pushed for lower fares on international routes, believing that when deregulation came, it would do better than most at working in a deregulated climate. The company had been adept at getting political concessions from a number of countries, but its very success was earning it a predatory reputation. However, it also underestimated the strength and determination of some of the European carriers, and market penetration was slower than planned.

8.   *Stakeholders. Which groups and individuals are affected by the way we do business? How do we establish win-win relationships with our stakeholders?* The airline had a good relationship with its banks, a fair relationship with its stockholders, and a poor relationship with its unions. Something that approached a win-win relationship with the pilots', flight attendants', and mechanics' unions was essential. The airline was accustomed to using its muscle instead of negotiating and engaging in conflict management.

9.   *Critical Resources. Which strategic resources, such as people, raw materials, technology, brain power, and so forth, do we need to do business? What are we doing to ensure a steady supply of these resources?* The airline needed to refurbish its fleet. Aging aircraft had to be replaced as quickly as possible by quieter, more flexible, and fuel-efficient planes that projected a much better image to customers. In the short term the company realized it did not have enough qualified aircraft to cover all the international routes it wanted to serve. Its growing reputation as a tough player positioned it well with the investment community. Money for new aircraft was readily available.

The subtasks just outlined fall into three groups: (1) the "mission, vision, values" group, which provides basic direction;

(2) the "markets, competencies, and products and services" group, which translates this basic direction into market terms; and (3) the "business environment, stakeholders, and strategic resources" group, which describes the larger environment—the "soup," so to speak—in which the entire enterprise floats. These subtasks, the building blocks of strategy, as it were, are illustrated in Figure 3.1. In the center of the figure is the desired outcome: focus and direction for the system. The loose structure of the design is intentional. Other "globes" can be added.

Once a company or institution does the fact-finding and analysis in each relevant subtask, the findings need to be integrated into a strategy—"our way forward"—together with strategic goals—"here are the major things we want to accomplish over the next one, two, three, four, or five years." The airline, for instance, in its striving to become a world-class carrier, de-

Figure 3.1. The Subtasks of Strategy.

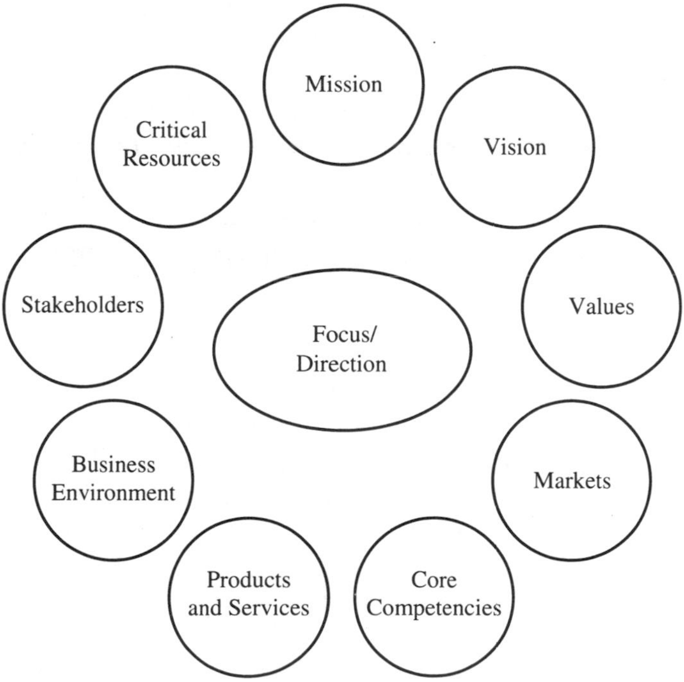

termined to establish at least two strategic partnerships with foreign airlines in order to begin the process of establishing foreign hubs.

Making Strategy Permeate the Enterprise

The strategy, once formulated, does not work automatically. Once it is formulated and tested, the managers of the company must make sure that it is cascaded through every unit within the institution, must sell it to every worker, must implement it, and must contribute to its fine-tuning. The strategy must permeate the institution.

The Strategy of Subunits. One way to cascade the overall strategy of a company down through all units and functions is to make sure that each unit has its own mission statement and ultimately its own strategy, derived from and linked to the company strategy. In Amoco Corporation each of the major subsidiaries has its own mission and strategy, and functional units have their own mission and strategy derived from and linked to the strategy of the corporation.

The president of the apparel division of a large retailer came from a meeting in which the new strategy of the company was announced and said to his troops, "It's now clear what we have to do. First of all, we must assimilate this strategy document; we must fully understand its purpose and implications. We have to make it come alive for ourselves. Second, we must take it and translate it into a strategy for apparel. We have to have our own strategy and make it come alive in our stores." The job of the president of the apparel division was not just to make money, but to make money through this new strategy, for it was the new strategy that would properly position the company in the industry and the marketplace and ensure not only its survival but its growth.

Strategy as Integrator of Operations. Operations, the focus of the next master task, deals with the day-to-day work of the system that leads to the delivery of products or services to customers.

The system is imbued with the strategy to ensure that strategy is continually providing focus and direction for the various operations found in the subunits of the company or institution. In larger companies with a number of departments or units, each unit has its own set of operations. Each unit has its own "business," as it were, its own set of internal or external customers, and its own set of work programs through which products and services are delivered to these customers.

For instance, while General Motors designs, manufactures, and sells automobiles, its human resources department is, among other things, in the "business" of recruiting, training, and developing the people who do this work. Getting the right people in the right jobs, or helping line managers do so, is a human resources "business" outcome that contributes substantially to the overall business outcomes of GM itself. The same can be said of marketing, finance, research and development, engineering, public and government affairs, manufacturing, and all the other units, functions, departments, and divisions of the company. The business of each unit must ultimately contribute to the principal business outcomes of the entire system. Strategy serves as the principal integrator of the work of the system. The purpose of strategy, as we have seen, is to provide focus and direction. But the best strategy in the world will not do this unless it gets into the guts of the system, that is, unless it drives both business operations and organizational processes and procedures. In too many companies, as we have seen, strategy "floats on the top," as it were, because a methodology for ensuring that strategy is at the heart of the system has not been formulated and executed.

Thinking Strategically About Operations. One of the impediments to the translation of strategy into operations is the lack of strategic thinking on the part of those responsible for operations. Often operations people will say, somewhat wistfully, "I wish that I had time just to sit and think about the business or to sit around with the team and just talk about the business." That is, day-to-day operations crowd out strategic thinking. It may be that some operations people do not have their priorities

straight. It may be essential to seize time to think and talk about
the business, or the problem might go a bit deeper. In my experience, it is more likely that operations personnel will think
operationally about the company strategy, which is good as far
as it goes, but not think strategically about operations. They
say, "Since our strategy calls for growth, how can I get 5 percent more this coming year?" This is good operational thinking. In fact, thinking in terms of constant incremental improvement is always good thinking. However, they do not tend to
say, "Using the strategy as a catalyst, how can I rethink and
reset the operations of this unit in order to get an immediate
25 percent increase?" In a company or institution committed
to constant improvement, thinking strategically about operations is a way of increasing value-added options.

A No-Formula Approach to Setting Strategy

You may find that for your business some of the subtasks outlined earlier are not that important. Or you may find that some
of the strategic considerations or subtasks that are important
for your business have been left out. That is easily solved by
adding them.

   Model A provides a template you can use to fashion your
own business. You must cast it in a form that makes sense for
you. There is no one right way of formulating a strategy. It is
more important to keep in mind the purpose of the strategy—
to provide longer-term focus and direction for the enterprise.
"Longer-term," of course, will mean different things to different companies and institutions. What is longer-term for Royal
Dutch/Shell would be an eternity for some high-tech companies.

   Model A provides the basic principles for designing, con-
structing, running, and assessing a system. What it does not
provide are simple formulas for success. There are three reasons for this no-formula approach. First, excellence is a moving target. Formulas that work today may have the opposite
effect tomorrow. Second, while there are general principles for
the pursuit of excellence, each company, institution, enterprise,
agency, functional unit, project, program, or task force must

apply these principles to its own peculiar set of circumstances, both internal and external. Each must not only find its own formulas but, as time goes by and circumstances change, reformulate them, that is, come up with a revised set that responds to the ever-changing environment. Third, as both theory and practice demonstrate, there are many different routes to success. One company is successful because it sticks to its knitting and creates a niche for itself in a focused market, while another finds success in developing different and unrelated businesses in a variety of markets. The former knows how to leverage niche creation into success; the latter knows how to leverage complexity.

Finding the right strategic formula calls for *Pareto thinking,* that is, determining which strategic elements will add the most value to the enterprise. Which high-priority issues should we focus on? Is finding the right markets the most important issue for us? Or is getting the right product mix? All companies and institutions must beware of finding the talisman for success they have long been looking for in any one of the master tasks or subtasks of Model A. There is no necessary linear relationship between any given task or subtask and success. Coming up with a new strategy does not automatically set an institution on the right path. Selecting the right markets is a step in the right direction, but success is woven from many threads. The message here is that most companies and institutions can be better than they are. Model A sends managers on a systematic search for both the causes of stagnation in their enterprises and for ways of moving ahead.

Master Task Two: Operations

The centerpiece of operations, indeed of Model A itself, is the manufacture and delivery of specific products or the design and delivery of services that meet the needs and wants of external or internal customers. The guiding principle is this:

Master Task Two: Deliver valued products and services cost effectively to customers.

The "sacred" moment in operations is the moment when the needs and wants of a customer are actually satisfied — for instance, the moment when the customer drives her new car out the door of the dealer's showroom, or the moment when the passenger gets off the airplane after a flight from New York saying to himself, "Now that was a good flight," or the sense of religious joy people experience when they participate in a meaningful liturgical ceremony. It is the same with internal customers. Some units within an organization provide products and services exclusively for internal customers. The "sacred" moment is the moment the manager leaves the human resource training seminar better equipped to carry out the performance management system or the moment when the logistics group gets the merchandise to the stores intact and on time for the weekend sale.

Operations are effective only to the degree that they lead to consistent delivery of need-satisfying products and services to customers. Some companies start out well but cannot hold the course. Both People's Express, the upstart airline, and Osborne Computer, an early player in the PC market, started out well but ended poorly. They both seemed to know what their respective markets wanted at the time they started their businesses. That is, their strategic intent was right. But they were not able to create operational systems that could meet the demand smoothly, effectively, and efficiently. Competitors gobbled them up. People's Express also made some strategic mistakes. The company tried to expand too rapidly, and this further complicated operational glitches. Here was an airline that professed from the start its total dedication to the needs of the customer and to the quality of work life of its employees but ended up failing both.

The Subtasks of Operations

Nine operations subtasks are considered here. While these are the generic operational tasks found in most companies and institutions, other tasks may need to be added for a given enterprise. The example used here involves a mass merchandiser turned specialty retailer. Retailing is a fast-moving business.

In the 1980s successful companies such as The Gap and The Limited did not do retailing; they created it.

1.   Customer Focus. *How effectively do we stay in touch with the changing needs and preferences of our customers? How well do our units understand the needs of their internal customers?* During its turnaround, the specialty retailer examined here had to change its focus from the goods being sold to the wants of its customers. This involved a culture change. Since different stores served different ethnic groups, the company had to learn how to match the goods to the store. A renewed customer focus helped the company exploit these local niches. The company wanted to attract new, younger customers. The question was, What do we need to be and do in order to maintain our current customer base and still get new ones?

2.   Specific Products and Services. *How effective is our product and service development process? How well are our products and services received by our customers? How do they compare to those of our competitors?* The retailer had to move from staid proprietary to national brands in order to retain old customers and draw in new ones. This meant convincing vendors that a "new" company was emerging, one that deserved to carry name brands. In its apparel business, the company had to develop proprietary brands to complement the new name brands. In its electronics business it had to breathe new life into still viable older brands.

3.   Work Design and Flow. *How effective, efficient, and humane are our work programs? Which need to be redesigned? What can we do to eliminate unnecessary work and streamline value-added work?* The retailer did a value analysis of all the activities in every department. By tracking goods from initial buying decision to final sale, it discovered activities that did not connect with one another, previously unnoticed bottlenecks, and a great deal of duplication of effort. Useless activities were jettisoned and the path of goods from vendor to customer was streamlined. Value analysis and streamlined work programs led to the elimination of millions of dollars of unneeded cost.

4.   Quality Assurance. How effective is our quality assurance strategy and plan? What do we need to do to improve quality? What do we have to do to establish a "culture" of quality? The retailer upgraded the quality of its proprietary brands. Brands with a "discount" feel were eliminated. "Get rid of junk wherever it's found" was the cry. "Buy quality goods that reflect the specialty store strategy" was the order of the day. In the beginning the company stopped doing the wrong things and then gradually began to do the right things. It began to gain a national reputation as a "value" retailer of quality goods at a reasonable price.

Reinventing their business

5.   Research and Development. What kind of innovators are we? To what degree is "constant improvement" part of our culture? How effectively do we turn creative ideas into value-added action? The retailer used both internal and external focus groups to generate ideas for doing everything within the company better. Competitor stores were shopped extensively and the best practices borrowed and adapted. Retailers that were on the edge but were not direct competitors — those at both the high end and at the low end — were studied and lessons were gathered. Since dozens of retailers were falling by the wayside, time was spent studying the causes of their failures. The company wanted to become a leader, a company creating rather than merely doing retailing in its own niche. It wanted to do what no other retailer had done well — become good at selling both soft goods such as apparel and hard goods such as appliances and electronics. Another group at the company were looking for acquisitions. The company was profitable and needed to find ways of leveraging its profits.

6.   Marketing. How well do we translate our marketing strategy into action? What kinds of images do our products and services have? How well do we promote them? How effectively do we distribute them? The retailer wanted to get rid of its dowdy discount store image. It faced a dilemma. Its "crowded" approach to newspaper advertising — too many items squeezed on a page — reinforced the discount store feel. This approach did nothing to improve the image of the company, but it did bring in a lot of customers. On the other hand, although customers liked the large, uncrowded look of some of the company's new ads and sales of advertised items soared, volume suffered. The company had to strike a balance between the new look in advertising and drawing in customers to buy a wide range of goods. Money was invested in TV ads, and these contributed greatly to the company's new image.

7. Customer Service. To what extent do we have a realistic customer service strategy? How effective are our frontline people? To what extent do we get feedback from customers and use it? How would our customers currently describe us? Realizing that few retailers provided high-quality customer service, the company established and communicated a thoughtful customer service strategy. In this industry, high-quality customer service can provide a competitive edge. A customer service strategy was formulated and promulgated. But the older poor service culture persisted. Part of the problem was failure to invest in service improvement programs. While the company could be a value retailer only if it contained costs, the cost-containment plank of the strategy at times stood in the way of the new image the company was desperately trying to create. Customer service had to be seen as an investment rather than a cost.

8. Material Resources. To what degree do we have the material resources we need to get our work done? How efficiently do we use them? To what degree do we streamline work before automating it through computers? The company gradually introduced new information management systems. New systems were needed to improve logistics and inventory management. As with other retailers, one of the biggest customer complaints was out-of-stock sale items. Making inroads here involved people, logistics, and systems. Data integrity was a problem; the computer showed that an item was in stock and the customer was told at the merchandise pickup area that it was not. The company also launched a store improvement program. Every store needed a look in line with the new image the retailer was trying to create.

9. Financial Management. How well do we manage such financial realities as cash flow? To what degree are realistic budgets established and implemented? How effectively do we control our costs? How "friendly" and balanced are our financial controls? The retailer excelled here. Excellent financial terms had been negotiated at the time of the management buyout—no junk bond financing—and, as interest rates fell, new terms were negotiated for outstanding debt. The company prided itself on tight budgets and effective controls. Unfortunately, this control mentality locked many people into the older view of retailing. Somehow the company had to move toward more friendly business-enhancing controls. Very tight budgets did not always serve the business.

These tasks together with the outcome realized by performing them well—satisfied customers, customers who come back for more—are shown in Figure 3.2. As noted earlier, subtasks can be added, deleted, or moved around to suit the needs of the business.

Figure 3.2. The Subtasks of Operations.

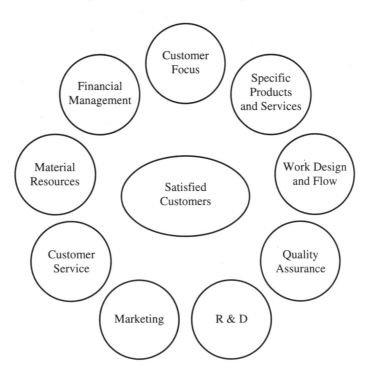

Operational success is often a question of doing many things well. Consider the following example. The Ford Taurus plant outside Atlanta was as productive as its counterparts in Japan (Eisenstein, 1991; Flint, 1991). This plant had discovered its own formula for success even though few could put their finger on just what the formula was: not a new plant, but one judiciously revamped for increased productivity; not a high-tech, robotized operation, but some robots in a clean, uncluttered, well-run plant; not a gung-ho young work force, but a mature group with a 35 percent minority makeup who understood quite well the fiercely competitive nature of the automobile business; a union plant where union leaders knew that cooperation was not the same as compromise, leading to an unusual sense of common purpose among unions, workers, and managers, all with a sense of ownership; not a state-of-the-art, just-in-time inventory system, but reduced inventories kept within bounds; not a Baldridge National Quality Award winner, but workers who relentlessly hunted down the causes of defects and eliminated them, drastically reducing the number of cars in the repair section; not high-impact teams, but excellent coordination stemming in part from the establishment of the role of "zone improvement person"; not a place that had explicitly formulated its own culture and preached the "Ford Atlanta Way," but a place with a strong culture that emphasized constant incremental improvement in a whole host of "little things" that added up to significantly improved productivity and a social system in which pride in getting the work done took precedence over standing around gassing.

In sum, it was a complex, not completely understood formula, but one that was theirs and one that worked. Given the success in Atlanta, the Chicago Taurus plant, also a low-tech operation, began emulating its sibling.

FOUR

Creating an Organization
That Serves the Business

Master Tasks Three and Four focus on the organizational dimensions of Model A. Typically, the word *organization* is used to refer to the entire company or institution. Here, however, it refers basically to organization structure — the boxes on the chart, if you will — and human resource management systems. People are deployed in the structure to do the work; together with their supervisors, they use human resource management systems to make sure that human resource realities serve the business.

An Advanced Organizer: What Chapter Four Is About

- *Master Task Three: Structure.* Create a structure that serves the business by optimizing information sharing, decision making, and work flow. The subtasks of structure include the macrostructure tasks of dividing labor among organizational units, aligning and coordinating the work of these units, establishing effective interunit communication, and promoting interunit teamwork. They also include the microstructure tasks of developing business-enhancing roles and jobs within units, cultivating interunit relationships, establishing effective intraunit communication, and promoting intraunit teamwork.

48

- *Master Task Four: Human Resource Management Systems.* Establish the kinds of human resource management systems that managers can use to develop a committed and productive workforce. The subtasks of human resource management include developing the following items: a human assets framework and audit process; a business-enhancing incentive and reward system; an effective recruitment system; a plan for socializing new hires into the organizational strategy and culture; an approach to human resource utilization; a flexible people development system; a system of career paths; a win-win approach to labor relations; and an effective retention and separation process.

Master Task Three: Structure

Structure deals with the division of labor among units and among individuals within units and the coordination and reintegration of the work once it is divided up. Structure provides conduits through which the work of the system flows. The principle is easy to state, more difficult to execute:

Master Task Three: Create a structure that serves the business by optimizing information sharing, decision making, and work flow.

Poor or inappropriate structures reduce productivity and add cost rather than value by impeding information sharing, decision making, and work flow.

The Subtasks of Structure

Structure provides answers to two critical questions: How should we divide up the work? And once the work is divided up, how do we reintegrate and coordinate it? There are two kinds of structure through which work flows: macrostructure and microstructure.

Macrostructure: Organizational Units. *Macrostructure* refers to establishing units or functions within the company or institution. The logic is simple: once the business agenda is in order, establish the kinds of organizational units needed to deliver strategic and operational business outcomes directly or to support their delivery. It should be noted, however, that since everything in Model A is "happening all at once," the business tasks and subtasks have a logical rather than a temporal priority over organizational tasks. Although business and organizational activities go hand in hand, organizational functions must serve business priorities.

There are four subtasks relating to macrostructure. The case focus is on an automobile manufacturing company. The aspects examined include a number of organizational changes that have been introduced over the past years by the Big Three automakers in their pursuit of Japanese competitors. While these companies have made great strides in improving quality and getting their organizations to serve their business better, foreign automotive firms have not rested on their laurels. U.S. manufacturers are chasing a moving target. In the section that follows, instead of asking a series of assessment questions as was the case with the first two master tasks, guiding principles for each subtask are outlined.

1. Division of Labor Among Organizational Units. Divide up the work by establishing organizational units with clear roles and responsibilities. Make sure that each unit has the authority needed to discharge its responsibilities. In this case example, the auto manufacturer created an entirely new company to launch a new car. It did so in order to develop a new culture of quality and flexibility. Furthermore, plagued in its other divisions by look-alike models, the company restructured its automotive divisions and gave them more autonomy to develop distinctive products. Over a three-year period the company got rid of over ten layers of management. Bureaucratic obstacles quickly disappeared, and the savings from this streamlining went straight to the bottom line. The company eliminated a strategic planning unit located for some reason in the human resources department. This unit produced reports that senior managers never read.

2. Organizational Geometry and Coordinating Mechanisms. Align the organizational units in a basic geometry that facilitates work. Then establish the kinds of coordinating mechanisms that will facilitate strategic and operational outcomes. Establish friendly controls. The automotive company fashioned a new strategy and used the strategy as the principal coordinating mechanism among its various units—design, engineering, manufacturing, marketing, human resources, and the rest. Every unit was expected to understand the company strategy, create its own strategy based on it, and list the strategic interfaces with other companies. Units with a history of being at odds with one another had to draw up a charter for working together. The warring units had to identify areas of difficulty and disagreement and then brainstorm ways of overcoming them. The final charter listed both agreed-upon goals and ways of achieving them. Finally, a matrix organization, considered by many as too cumbersome to work well, was established for the design and development of new cars. The president of the company admitted the difficulties with the structure but said it was the only one that ensured the kind of cooperation needed among the units involved. The time needed to produce a new model dropped from six to three years.

3.   Interunit Communication. Develop and consistently use interunit communication processes and practices such as information sharing, feedback, problem solving, innovation-focused dialogue, and conflict management that make the structure serve the business. The automaker came to the realization that, since managers were drowning in information, they often failed to focus on what was most important. Efforts were made to cut down drastically on information flow. The company also established an internal supplier-customer approach to communication in which every functional unit was a supplier or customer with respect to other units. Customers no longer had to mindlessly accept the products or services provided by another. If an internal supplier did not provide products or services that met quality, price, and delivery time standards, the customer was allowed to look outside. Feedback from customers to suppliers became the order of the day. When a supplier unit and a customer unit disagreed on the quality of a product or service offered, they used a simple negotiation process to iron out their differences. Manufacturing and marketing set up regular "focus on innovation" groups.

4.   Interunit Teamwork. Establish a climate of teamwork among the units to ensure that they relate to one another as suppliers and customers. Since neither structure nor coordinating mechanisms work by themselves, the people within the units must make them work. Making them work well or even superbly is called teamwork. The automaker was not satisfied with "decent" relationships among key interacting units. Every unit with a stake in the design and development of a new model or a new car, including the design, engineering, manufacturing, finance, marketing, and sales groups, had at least one member on every new-product team. With the new team approach, units began to anticipate the needs of the units with which they interacted. The company's credit services division reorganized itself into multifunctional teams. Customers received faster, better service, and productivity soared.

Microstructure: Structure Within Organizational Units. Micro-structure refers to the jobs, roles, responsibilities, and accountabilities that people have as they work within the subunits of the macrostructure. For instance, in the training unit of the human resources department there is a training manager together with training needs assessment specialists, technical training design specialists, technical skills trainers, organization development training design specialists, organization development trainers, and management development trainers. The four subtasks of microstructure are outlined as follows.

1.   Business-Enhancing Jobs and Roles. Establish flexible jobs, roles, and positions that clearly add value to the business; give people the authority and flexibility they need to accomplish business-enhancing goals. The automaker negotiated with the unions to introduce greater job flexibility into the workplace. This was relatively easy to do in the new car venture, but the unions were more recalcitrant in the older divisions. However, in the end, workers were cross-trained on two or three different jobs. They actually enjoyed the variety, with some actively pursuing job rotation. Also, since manufacturing technology was changing rapidly, the company negotiated the option to add new jobs and eliminate others in the plants. Current employees were given the opportunity to develop skills needed for the new technology. In its R&D unit, the company experimented with skills matrices that specified competencies and levels of performance rather than job descriptions or jobs-in-a-box. Through these matrices employees began to see what they could contribute to increased productivity while ensuring their own career success.

2.   Intraunit Relationships. Establish within each unit the kind of working relationships — a working geometry — that maximizes the potential of workers and the value-added work flow in the delivery of strategic and operational outcomes. Since interdependencies among workers, however fluid and shifting, are central to the work of organizational units, the automaker saw the need for establishing coordinating mechanisms, not just between units, but also between people with different jobs within the same unit. People within the R&D function were often working on several projects at the same time. Strategic priorities established by the vice president of research and his senior team constituted one of the key coordinating mechanisms. For instance, the design and manufacture of a brand-new car body that used 50 percent more plastic than other models demanded that a metals specialist and a plastics specialist work together. For workers to be able to live with the give-and-take of these interdependencies was not enough for the company; it wanted them to learn and grow from them.

3.   Intraunit Communication. Ensure that every worker has the incentives, skills, and technology needed to engage in the kind of information sharing, feedback, problem solving, innovation-focused dialogue, and conflict management that adds value to the work of the unit. Make sure that intraunit communication serves improved work flow and business outcomes. The automaker discovered that one of the principal reasons quality programs failed was a lack of communication skills among workers. People failed to listen carefully to one another; workers did not know how to challenge others to prevent mistakes. The company experimented in simple communication skills training programs that used workplace examples to highlight essential skills. The workplace became the lab where employees were to practice these skills. As with the simple statistical process skills needed to track quality, workers were expected to become competent in basic communication skills. In the plant manufacturing the new car, peer feedback programs together with an upward evaluation sysem were introduced. Problem solving was also emphasized. Once the workers learned a relatively simple problem-solving process, problem solving began to replace blaming.

4.   Intraunit Teamwork. Develop team spirit within the unit. Promote both teamwork and individual initiatives when they make business sense. Self-managed teams with cross-trained workers were used wherever possible. Often enough these teams redesigned work programs, making them more efficient. To ensure accountability, the company required status reports on key projects to be routinely shared with the manager of the unit within which the self-managed team was working. The give-and-take of these sessions reinforced rather than cast doubt on the work of the teams. Productivity in the company began to rise, and because of improved relations between workers and management, morale improved. Team members began to see other auto manufacturers — not management and coworkers — as their real competitors. Despite the major focus on teams, individual initiative was still encouraged. People who did not fit in with a team approach switched to jobs that did not involve close interaction with others. They still saw themselves as members of the larger team, however, and they were still suppliers who had to respond to their internal customers' requirements. Plants adopting the team approach, both between and within units, were 30 percent more productive than traditional plants, costs were lower, and absenteeism and turnover were significantly lower.

The eight subtasks of macrostructure and microstructure are illustrated in Figure 4.1. Note that the outcome is "an organization that serves the business." Another way to state the desired outcome is "optimized information sharing, decision making, and work flow." The structures are means to an end, not an end in themselves.

Figure 4.1. The Subtasks of Structure.

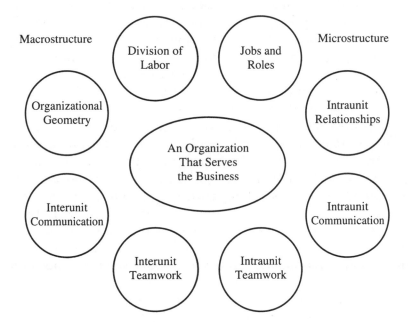

No Formula for Designing Structure

There is general agreement among the experts that there is no single best way to structure an organization. The overall principle is clear — structure should serve strategy and strategy-driven operations — but the application of this principle depends on the specific set of circumstances in which any given company or institution finds itself. One company may need to centralize to optimize productivity, while another may need to decentralize. Some companies stick to tried-and-true structures. Others opt for new-look structures with names such as "network" or "shamrock." Still others claim that structure is a thing of the past and the best structure is a minimalist one. Again, the principles are clear: get a reasonable structure and make it serve the business.

While there is no ideal way to design a structure, it is still possible to construct a faulty one. As late as 1992 the chief of design and the head of research at General Motors reported to the head of research and development. In turn the R&D head reported to the person running the aerospace and computer divisions. The result: GM was developing new technologies quickly but was slow to apply them, and new-product development was slow and costly. It was a case of a structure not serving the business. In Britain in 1991 the board of the BBC named a director-general designate. At the same time, for whatever personal or political reasons, they extended the term of the incumbent for eighteen months. The principal business need of the BBC at the time was to reformulate strategy to take into account the massive changes in both radio and television, which were having a profound impact on broadcasting, and to restructure the organization to better serve the new strategy. Meeting these needs was next to impossible: the lame duck was not going to reformulate strategy, and the director-general designate could not, at least not publicly. Another case of a structure, however temporary, that did not serve the business, this one led to constant uncertainty and turmoil within the organization and was not resolved until the end of 1992.

Restructuring

It is impossible to pick up a business publication without reading about one or more companies' restructuring. While this term can be used in a variety of ways, here it means changing the macrostructure or microstructure as outlined in this chapter. Some companies change their structures constantly, for at least two reasons. First, they change because they are in volatile businesses such as the computer industry. New structures are called for to meet the changing environment and changing customer demands. The more turbulent the environment, the more rapid the pace of change in organizational structures. Second, some companies change structure frequently because they see reorganizing as a way of keeping people on their toes. Then the issue becomes the trade-off between stability—When will all of this stop so we can get on with our work?—and having an organization that enhances rather than limits the business. The first question for a company restructuring should be, What are our needs and how will a new structure make the business better? This is not just a good question, but the crucial question. If a company has a poor strategy, a new structure is not the remedy. Business problems need business answers.

Organizing to Serve the Business: Reality Versus Theory

A primary working principle of Model A is that the business should drive the organization and, conversely, the organization should serve the business. As most of us know, however, this principle is not always honored. Consider educational systems and government agencies. Since these institutions receive funding regardless of their effectiveness and efficiency, some of them tend to pursue organizational agendas at the expense of business outcomes. In the case of education systems, students do not learn and develop as they might because teachers and administrators, those who run the institution, are often preoccupied with their own concerns rather than those of students. Moreover, the ballooning of the educational bureaucracy in primary and secondary schools has cast them in the business of surviving rather than of delivering services to customers — that is, their students.

In the world of education and government, politics often dictate organizational structure. For instance, while decentralization may make more educational sense in some areas, centralized structures are established because they make more "pork barrel" sense. Rarely do such institutions consider the kinds of structure they need to help students learn, grow, and develop more effectively. This is not to suggest that in for-profit enterprises the organization always serves the business. But unlike churches, government agencies, and educational institutions, for-profit institutions disappear if their organizations are not structured to meet the needs of the businesses they serve.

Master Task Four:
Human Resource Management Systems

However important structure may be, even more important are the people deployed in the structure, the people who fill the roles, jobs, and positions, the people who make the structure work and deliver the goods. The principle, then, reads thus:

Master Task Four: Establish the kinds of human resource management (HRM) systems that managers can use to develop a committed and productive workforce.

Every company and institution wants a committed and productive workforce, but some fail to take HRM seriously.

Taking Human Resource Management Seriously

Though there are still many run-of-the-mill personnel departments, human resource (HR) planning and development has come to be recognized as a critical function, and the person heading that department sits with the other decision makers of the company. In many, if not most, companies, people constitute a strategic resource. Before the recession of the early 1990s, in certain parts of the country, such as the Northeast, many fast food outlets could not grow because they could not find the people to staff them. In many countries around the world businesses suffer because they cannot find locally the kind of people they need, especially managerial talent. But human resources are just one of many critical resources. People resources must be aligned with such resources as money, technology, space, time, and information.

On a more operational level, different people have different needs and must be managed or supervised differentially. Young workers and older workers have different needs. For instance, when given the choice, younger and older workers choose different items from a menu of benefits. Tailored supervision can help people give their best. Furthermore, putting the people with the right set of skills in the right jobs can contribute greatly to a company's success. On the other hand, the wrong person in the wrong place can inhibit the productivity of an entire work unit. Human resource planning is needed to pull all of this together, starting with a human resources strategy that parallels and serves the business strategy. Companies that manage their human resources effectively have a distinct competitive edge.

Many companies do not manage their human resources well, either strategically or operationally. Time after time in organization after organization, managers or HR practitioners hire problematic people, keep them, fail to develop them, eventually promote them, and then try to manage the backwash from all this. People can be problematic for a variety of reasons: they lack requisite skills and the ability to develop them, they are "difficult" people with histories of poor interpersonal relationships, they are not self-starters and therefore need a great deal of supervision, they are not team players in settings where teamwork is essential, they propagate the politics of self-interest, they are not flexible and do not adapt easily to change, and so on. When it comes to values, they are dishonest or do not buy into the positive values that guide the organization. While every organization makes mistakes in hiring from time to time, good ones have the courage to correct their mistakes. The best companies establish HR procedures not only to manage such problems but also to prevent them. More than that, since they really believe that people are their most important resource, they establish comprehensive and viable HR policies and management systems and implement them consistently, guided by their people-oriented mission, vision, and values.

The Subtasks of Effective Human Resource Management

If managers are to manage people well, or better yet, facilitate workers' pursuit of business-enhancing goals, they need to have a practical set of HRM systems. Effective managers understand the HR needs of the business. All nine subtasks of effective HRM focus on establishing the kinds of HRM systems that managers and supervisors can use to help people give their best.

The case illustrations for the HRM master tasks deal with the HRM needs of an international agricultural research center.

1.   A Human Assets Framework and Audit Process. Establish a human assets audit process to take stock of the human resources of the institution. The agricultural research center discovered that it kept a strict account of every penny spent and every bit of inventory but knew comparatively little about its workforce. A system was set up so that each supervisor could place each worker on some kind of audit chart, indicating the person's strengths, weaknesses, and special talents. This initial audit, which was to be developed into an ongoing process, immediately pinpointed both skill and productivity deficits that would stand in the way of implementing the center's new strategy. Managers also learned that HR accounting has nothing to do with "slavery," as some of its critics had suggested. In fact, without such a process inequities in dealing with employees that damaged morale were much more likely to occur. By using an audit process, the center discovered that there was much more expertise inside the institution than anyone had realized. The expertise of people was overlooked because it was not reflected in the job descriptions or was not needed to do a particular job.   HAY

2.   *Incentives and Rewards. Establish the kind of incentive and reward systems that promote both productivity and high-quality work life.* The incentive/reward system needs to serve the business. The agricultural research center thought that, especially inasmuch as it was a not-for-profit organization, it was important for its managers to understand the basic principles of human motivation and how these principles translate into business-enhancing supervisory behavior. The center discovered that it was "incentives poor." It had been assumed that everyone considered it a privilege to work there and that everyone was a self-starter. Pay incentives were established for those who undertook distasteful but essential field work. Supervisors who had come to think of their workers as lazy discovered to their dismay that there were often more rewards for not working than for working. The system, not the workers, was at fault. The center, after studying the pros and cons, offered raises to workers who learned new, business-related skills. Job satisfaction, productivity, and quality of technical services all improved.

3.   *Recruitment. Hire people who have the working knowledge, skills, and attitudes needed to do the job or who can be cost-effectively trained to do so.* The center learned the hard way that hiring the right

people saves endless grief later on. They had no hiring system, especially for managers and administrators, and practically no one had a good set of interviewing skills. The center's hiring mistakes proved costly. The most costly errors involved people who refused to leave even after it became clear that the center was not the place for them. The center established recruitment policies and a system to implement them. Since in many cases attitudes were more important than skills—for instance, willingness to contribute to science by making sure that good science took place by supervising other scientists rather than merely doing one's own research—the institution adopted a policy of "hiring attitudes." It found it easy to provide skills but difficult to change attitudes. The center began hiring people for the institution itself and its preferred culture, rather than just for a particular job.

4.   Socialization. Socialize newcomers into the business and into a culture that supports both strategy and operations and key strategic drivers such as quality and customer service. This assumes, of course, that the institution has a culture that serves the business. The agricultural research center did have such a culture, or at least they knew what they wanted that culture to be. At the center it became everyone's job to help socialize new hires or old-timers moving into new jobs in the essence of the business and the preferred culture—"the way we do things here." A socialization system replaced pro forma orientation days and the handing out of personnel manuals. In the old culture new scientists were almost dared to be successful. Now it became everyone's job to do whatever was necessary to ensure the success of the newcomer.

5.   Utilization. Strive to maintain optimal staffing levels and continually try to put the right person in the right job, thereby enhancing both productivity and quality of work life. Managers at the agricultural research center learned that their units tended to be most productive when they were slightly understaffed. Somehow, everyone pulled together more effectively. Significant understaffing, on the other hand, created severe morale problems. They also learned that they could not put the right person in the right job without doing a human assets audit. The managers of the center kept a computer file on all the talents and special abilities of those who worked there. They used the file to put people in special projects, put together task forces, and decide whom to send to other centers on temporary assignment. Previously, even when it was clear that the wrong person had been put in the wrong job, managers at the center had been slow to correct their mistake. An attitude of the old culture persisted: people should endure what they do not like out of loyalty to the center.

6. *Development. Establish a process of ongoing development based on the needs of the business and the career focus of employees. Explore developmental strategies beyond formal training.* The agricultural research center defined development as "helping people become more valuable to the center and therefore more valuable to themselves." The institution, which had to do more and more with less and less, set its sights on creating a "culture of development" — everyone into self-development, every manager and supervisor a developer of people. A team of line managers and HR specialists brainstormed thirty different ways of developing people that they had seen used in this center and others. Unlike training, which is expensive, most of these approaches were free. Developing people was a strategic objective of the performance management system for all managers. The center did what most companies fail to do — it rewarded supervisors for developing people in ways that supported the mandate of the institution.

7. *Career Paths. Establish a career path system that contributes to both business outcomes and the quality of work life. Clarify the roles that both employees and managers are to play in implementing the system.* As in most institutions, the people at the center had worked under the caveat, If you are not in charge of your career, then no one is. Since the center had to do more with less, the key to a meaningful career path system lay in divorcing career paths from promotion: "Up is not the only way." The challenge facing a task force composed of managers and members of several em-

ployee committees was to devise a system to help people create
satisfying career paths that at the same time added value to the
center. The institution needed to designate company-enhancing
career "routes," that is, a job rotation system that balanced the
needs of workers with the needs of the center.

*Crosstraining
too*

8.   Labor Relations. *In nonunion institutions, work at fostering the
kind of work life that makes a union superfluous; in union institutions,
work toward a business-enhancing and worker-enhancing partnership.*
While the agricultural research center had no formal unions,
there was a range of employee associations and committees. After
a rocky start, the institution began to work toward win-win approaches. It took time to overcome the culture of paternalism
that permeated most management/worker relationships. The
center had developed a set of "people" values to complement
its business values. Grievances were responded to quickly, and
there was a much greater use of negotiation in settling disputes.
The institution came to realize that most of its workers were
just as committed to the high-quality and cost-effective execution of the center's mandate as senior managers and senior scientists were.

9.   Retention and Separation. *Establish viable HR retention and
separation systems and policies together with guidelines for implementing
them.* Since a considerable degree of downsizing was part of the
institution's response to the mandate to do more with less, separation procedures were critical. While most of the departures
took place through early retirement, voluntary separation, and
buyout programs, the center used restructuring as an opportunity to get rid of unproductive workers. With regard to those
who were fired, there was much less backlash than expected.
While the principal employee association made a lot of noise,
most workers who were staying were glad to see the detractors
and laggards go. For years they had resented having to work
harder because some did practically no work at all. One sour
note. The center failed to put in place creative retention programs. As a result, quite a few workers whom the center did
not want to lose left because of the attractiveness of the early

retirement and buyout programs. This was a costly mistake because their replacements had to be located, hired, and socialized into the system.

The HRM subtasks are illustrated in Figure 4.2. The
desired outcome is a robust workforce — skilled, savvy, committed, self-starting, and productive.

Now that we have reviewed the four master tasks of business and organizational effectiveness through the Model A
framework, we can turn our attention to the pragmatic concerns
of management and leadership. What kind of management and
leadership is necessary for companies and institutions to make
sure the needs of the business as outlined in these four master
tasks are met? Chapter Five examines Master Task Five, management, and Master Task Six, leadership.

Figure 4.2. The Subtasks of Effective Human Resource Management.

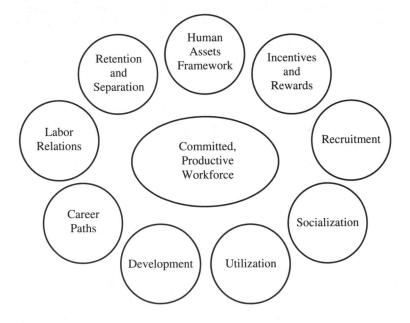

FIVE

The Pragmatics of
Management and Leadership

Chapters Three and Four deal with the strategic, operational, structural, and HRM needs of the business as outlined by Model A. Companies and institutions must also develop the kinds of systems needed to ensure a steady supply of good managers and leaders. These systems, though often receiving inadequate attention, are just as essential as strategic, operational, structural, and HRM systems. In this chapter, two more master tasks — setting up both management and leadership systems — are added to the Model A framework.

An Advanced Organizer: What Chapter Five Is About

- *Master Task Five: Value-Added Management.* Establish systems to develop a cadre of knowledgeable and skilled managers to identify and take care of the needs of the business. Managers add value by accomplishing business-enhancing objectives in the areas outlined in Figure 2.1. They also add value to the work of others through coordination, facilitation, and support.
- *Master Task Six: Pragmatic Leadership.* Develop leaders at every level of the organization to provide business-enhancing innovation and change. The essence of leadership is per-

formance beyond the ordinary. Leadership is about results, not charisma or other personality characteristics.

- *A summary of the uses of Model A.* A recap of the various ways managers can use Model A.

A question often asked is, Is there a difference between management and leadership? The answer given here is yes. However, managers can also be leaders. It depends on the results that managers achieve and how they achieve them. Moreover, as leadership is described here, factory floor workers can also be leaders.

Master Task Five: Value-Added Management

Now that the generic needs of the business have been reviewed, it is easier to see how managers can add value to the business. Once more the overall principle is clear:

Master Task Five: Establish systems to develop a cadre of knowledgeable and skilled managers to identify and take care of the needs of the business and to provide value-added supervision through coordination, facilitation, and support of the work of others.

Managers do two basic things: they manage processes and supervise people. Effective managers integrate the two in ways that increase productivity and improve quality of work life.

Managers as Managers of Processes

Here the word *processes* refers to all the master tasks and subtasks of Model A. The role of the manager as orchestrator of business-enhancing tasks or processes is to see to it that the principles of business and organizational effectiveness (described in Chapters Three and Four) are tailored to his or her institution or unit and consistently implemented. Therefore, when managers engage in strategic planning, set up a TQM program, arrange for more effective communication between their unit and another, redesign the roles in their units, establish management succession processes, or develop companywide employee participation programs in order to encourage leadership at every level of the institution, they are managing the processes of the institution. A marketing manager must see to it that an effective marketing plan, based on overall company strategy, is drawn up and implemented. A plant manager must see to it that quality is built into the company's work programs and products. A raw materials manager must establish the kind of relationships with suppliers that ensure the just-in-time flow of high-quality materials at reasonable prices. From an organizational point of view, the head of the intensive care department must see to it that the members of his or her team work together smoothly and efficiently toward patient survival and improvement. The head of the recruitment department of an investment bank must see to it that highly skilled investors who are compatible with the mission and philosophy of the institution and with the other members of the team are both recruited and socialized into the system. Managers are responsible for a wide range of outcomes that add value to the business. In sum, managers are developers, coordinators, and facilitators of all the tasks of Model A.

Managers as Supervisors of People

Managers, in their role as managers of people, are called supervisors. Supervisors are found at all levels of an organization. Sometimes the word *supervisor* is used to mean a manager at the lowest levels of the institution or some kind of team leader. Thus we say, "She was promoted from a supervisory to a managerial position." However, supervisiors in even this restricted sense usually do more than just manage people; they try to make some part of the institution work and are responsible for some of the subtasks identified in Model A. Therefore, in this book *manager* refers to anyone who has the responsibility for making some system or some part of a system work. If he or she must achieve goals through others, then he or she is also a supervisor.

Ideally, managers implement the principles of excellence through partnerships with the people they manage. Every good manager knows that without competent, motivated workers he

or she is dead in the water. Some managers are great at formulating strategy but awful at getting others to buy into the
strategy. This inability to deal with people effectively subverts
their strategy-related skills.

Finally, managers as supervisors use the HRM systems
reviewed in Master Task Four of Model A to carry out their
supervisory work. If these systems are missing or poorly designed, the quality of supervision will suffer.

The Subtasks of Value-Added Management

Managers are responsible for creating and installing effective
managerial systems. There is a problem with this. Managers,
immersed as they are in day-to-day operations, do not have time
left over to think about management itself. The eight subtasks
of value-added management constitute a framework for thinking about management itself.

The case focus here is a chemical company that is a division of a large energy corporation.

*1. Shared Managerial Framework. Develop a comprehensive, in-
tegrated system of management to provide a framework and a common
language for managing. Socialize all managers into the system.* As noted
earlier, many managers do not manage as well as they might
for two reasons: first, they do not have a blueprint for managing; second, they receive little feedback on how well they are
managing. To professionalize management, the chemical company developed a total quality management system for all managers. The company then used *360s,* feedback surveys designed
to give managers the feedback needed to improve. (The surveys are called 360s because feedback comes from all directions:
self, boss, peers, subordinates, and, at times, customers and suppliers. Since such massive feedback was countercultural, the
360s, at least for the first couple of years, were used for development rather than appraisal purposes.)

*2. Managerial Role Clarity. Make sure that all managers under-
stand their role and the key ways in which they can add value to the busi-*

ness. At the chemical company, managerial role clarity started with the CEO. The role of the president, a superb engineer and strategist, was widened to include communicating with the troops and rallying them around the new global strategy. Even though he preferred to engage in tasks that were directly related to the business, such as overseeing acquisitions and establishing strategic partnerships, he understood how important the cheerleader role was and had the skills for that job. With more effective information management systems in place, middle managers in the company had to reassess their roles. Information dissemination and control functions had to be rethought. In fact, all managers were asked to do an audit of their weekly activities against the background of the newly formulated management system, separating those activities that added relatively little value from those that added much value to the business. They used this audit to define a flexible managerial role for themselves that added more value. They fine-tuned this role in discussions with their bosses.

3.   Managers as Supervisors. *Choose managers who can use HRM to add value in terms of both productivity and quality of work life. Make sure that managers and supervisors have the interpersonal skills needed to supervise. Reward supervisors for developing people.* The chemical company first updated key HRM systems, including recruitment, socialization, development, and career path systems. Line managers were consulted as to how these systems could be linked to and add value to the business. Managers were chosen because they were good at working with and through others. Managers without the requisite communication skills were given some options for developing them. The company needed fewer controllers and more cheerleaders, especially in terms of rallying the troops around the new global strategy and getting people proactively involved in the new global structure. Managers who produced results but destroyed people in the process were first warned and then terminated.

4.   Performance Management System. *Develop a value-added performance management system that focuses on improving performance. Make* *sure the system is owned by both supervisors and those supervised. Eliminate all paperwork that does not add value.* The chemical company established a committee composed of line managers and a consultant to revamp the performance management system, turning it into one that focused mainly on performance rather than on appraisal and compensation. The committee turned the system into an instrument of strategy rather than one of day-to-day operations by making sure that key objectives, established through dialogue among managers and their direct reports, were strategic in nature. The system they were replacing encouraged not strategy but trivia. Some subordinates had over twenty "key" objectives, most of them relating to day-to-day operational issues for which they were already accountable. The company worked at creating a culture of feedback or of feedback loops so that both corrective and confirmatory response took place close to the relevant event. If the feedback system worked, then appraisal meetings would hold no surprises. The company trained literally hundreds of line managers to train others in the use of the system. The new system was to be a line system with the human resources department providing not leadership but support.

5.   Levels of Management. Establish only as many levels of management as needed to serve the business. Make sure that managers understand the roles of other managers and their relationships to them so that their work can be integrated. Like many other companies, the one in this example eliminated several layers of management through restructuring. Over the years layers of management had been created to provide career paths for successful managers. Since this retrenchment meant that the span of control of the average manager increased, managers had to hone their skills of delegation and find more focused ways of adding value through supervision. One manager found ways of adding value by helping self-managed teams work more effectively and efficiently. She ended up working as a consultant with a variety of teams at different levels. The company set up interlevel managerial meetings in which managers met with their boss and one key subordinate who was a manager in his or her own right. They discussed interlevel dynamics and brainstormed ways of improving collaboration. For instance, the vice president of marketing met with the director of sales and one of his key regional managers. They discovered that there was a great deal of overlap in the work they were doing. They also discovered that there were a lot of good ideas about marketing among sales representatives that never surfaced and got used.

6. *Selection of Managers.* *Choose managers on the basis of their potential to deliver the shared management system. Choose people who want to both manage and supervise.* At the chemical company people had been routinely promoted to managerial positions with little attention to their managerial qualifications. With the help of a consulting group, the company set up an internal assessment center to evaluate people being considered for promotion. This included people who were moving into managerial positions for the first time and those who were moving up. The assessment activities were based on the management system that had recently been installed. Since some highly creative workers were lacking in either managerial potential or the desire to manage, a technical promotion track was established to parallel the management track. Some people already in managerial positions chose to move to the technical track. Rectifying past mistakes in moving unqualified people into managerial roles proved to be stickier. When one manager was demoted two grades, there was a great deal of resentment even among those who thought that he should never have been chosen in the first place. Colleagues thought he was taking the blame for a poor management system.

7. *Development of Managers.* *Make sure that managers have the basic working knowledge and skills to work from the shared management system. Continually develop managers in order to help them improve their productivity and skills.* The chemical company wanted a management development system in place, not a mishmash of programs. And the system needed to be updated continually to factor in the changing needs of the business. For instance, when budgets were cut and the company was asked to downsize by about two thousand workers, a new set of skills were called for. The most important part of management development was the acquisition of skills needed in the new global marketplace — developing global product strategies, developing strategic alliances, putting in place global marketing strategies, global coordination and integration, global staffing and development, and creating a culture to support all of this. This meant revamping the curriculum at the recently opened management training center.

**8.   *Managerial Succession Planning.* *Make sure that there is a steady stream of people capable of assuming higher managerial and supervisory responsibilities. Reward managers for developing their successors.* For years management succession planning had been an afterthought at this chemical company. As a result, at the very time managers were needed for the company's new global strategic push, it could not find them inside; the company also had a culture that made it reluctant to look outside. It had to pass up an opportunity to acquire at a bargain price another company with an excellent strategic fit, because it did not have the managers to staff it. The company established new procedures whereby every manager had to help prepare two people who could succeed him or her. All managers who managed other managers were asked to engage in the following succession activities: make sure that their managers had not overlooked anyone with managerial potential; ensure that their managers understood the standards and criteria for choosing managers; check the qualifications of those considered to have high potential; make certain that their managers understood the career aspirations of those with high potential together with the corresponding career routes identified by the company; guarantee that management development plans were in place for managers with high potential; review the progress of high-potential managers with each of them; and match the upcoming management cadre with the needs of the organization.

These management system subtasks are illustrated in Figure 5.1. As in other areas of Model A, there are no pat formulas to be used. While the principles are clear — for instance, ensure that managers have the interpersonal skills needed for

Figure 5.1. The Subtasks of Value-Added Management.

effective supervision — each company and institution has to work out its own formula. For many companies, unfortunately, creating effective management systems is not high on the priority list.

The Performance Management System

The subtasks of management can be further divided into contributing skills and tasks. Performance management, together with the subtasks and skills it entails, is one of the most discussed and written-about systems. It is a managerial and supervisory system that involves continually helping those supervised improve their personal performance and thus the company's overall operation. It calls for some mix of planning, collaborative objective setting, delegation, work program development, work facilitation, two-way feedback between manager and direct report, monitoring of key performance outcomes, training and development, appraisal, and recognition and reward.

Few companies have effective performance management systems, so a brief overview of the issues involved in developing an innovative one is presented here. The guiding focus in establishing such a system should be, What needs to be done to make sure that the system adds value?

- *Cost center versus profit center.* Performance management systems are either profit centers or cost centers; they are never neutral. That is, they either contribute to improved individual performance and therefore add value, or they do not improve individual performance, in which case they are cost centers because time and other resources are consumed with nothing to show for the investment. Cost centers should be eliminated.
- *Strategy versus trivia.* The performance management system must reinforce strategy, not trivia. The system was never meant to govern everything a person does. It should be a Pareto system, one that focuses on those relatively few key (strategic) objectives that will add the most value to the business. Trivial objectives focusing on activities rather than strategy-related business-enhancing outcomes are, sadly, the norm.
- *Performance versus appraisal.* Some people incorrectly refer to performance management systems as appraisal systems. Appraisal is retrospective; it takes place after everything is over, as it were, when it's too late. Performance management is prospective; its entire purpose is not to appraise but to facilitate and improve performance.
- *Development versus control.* The performance management system should be a system for developing people rather than a system for control. Managers often present it as a control system, which immediately establishes a negative psychology around it.
- *Managers versus the human resources department.* Performance management is the responsibility of every manager. Handing over the performance management system to the human resources department for administration almost inevitably means that it becomes almost exclusively an appraisal system.

- *Managers' incentives.* Many managers hate the performance management system precisely because it is an exercise in trivia. Only when they experience it as adding value will they learn to love it. Designed and used properly, the system will simplify managers' lives and make their work easier. Most managers see the system as a burden. Among these, some see it as a necessary burden; others as simply a useless organizational ritual.
- *A bilateral versus unilateral system.* If workers see performance management as something that is done to them, as a tool for management to impose capricious or unreasonable quotas, for example, then it may well be doomed. At its best it is a collaborative process to improve the business. Ideally, performance management discussions are a double-loop learning process. Managers and their reports should constitute a problem-solving, innovation-focused team.

To see how managers can use the activities of performance management to energize instead of control employees, we return to the case of the mass merchandiser turned specialty retailer (discussed in Chapter Three under "The Subtasks of Operations").

- *Key objectives.* Company managers asked employees to help identify key strategy-related objectives. This was the first time since the company's turnaround that employees were asked to be contributors, and they responded with a wide range of innovative objectives. For instance, one store sales associate took on the task of determining where to relocate the merchandise checkout areas by exploring the flow of customer traffic and customer preferences.
- *Delegation and empowerment.* Managers asked employees how much responsibility they could handle. To their amazement they discovered that most employees thought that too little was asked of them, especially in terms of coming up with and executing ideas for improving the business.
- *Work programs.* Managers routinely spent time with employees brainstorming ways of meeting objectives. They usually ended up with better ideas than if either had worked alone. Employees who said, "Now that I know my key objectives, let me run with them," were encouraged to do so.

- *Facilitation.* Managers asked employees, "What can I do to help you accomplish your objectives?" The answers were quite inventive. One said, "I'd like to rearrange the merchandise pickup area, but the regional manager is going to get on my tail if he gets wind of it. I want you to run interference for me." The store manager did just that, and the new pickup arrangement was later adopted by the entire region.

- *The feedback loop.* Managers gave frequent feedback, both confirmatory and corrective, on key activities and outcomes, most of it informal. "Five-minuters" were the order of the day. Managers also encouraged feedback on their own activities and style from their direct reports. One manager who got little upward feedback discovered that although she verbally encouraged employees to give her feedback on her ideas and her style, nonverbally she discouraged people from doing so. Employees believed her nonverbal signals more than her words. It took one courageous employee to break through the impasse.

- *Monitoring.* The retailer's managers took monitoring to mean follow-up. When they gave corrective feedback, they followed up to see how things were going. Most employees took this to mean concern and interest rather than control. One employee asked, "Shouldn't we take the initiative for monitoring?" From that point on, many managers engaged in monitoring as an exception rather than as standard practice.

- *Development.* Because managers and direct reports had such good communication with one another in terms of meeting the needs of the business, it became clear to both what development activities would lead to improved productivity and quality of work life. One employee asked to work part-time in two departments that were having trouble coordinating their efforts. He thought that everyone in his department blamed those in the other for the problems. But he knew that there were two sides to the story. Working in both gave him the opportunity to learn the work of the other department and then to act as a liaison when the two got together to develop a charter for working with each other.

Of course, the full performance management process includes appraisal and compensation, but too often these are focused on at the expense of performance improvement. The retail company employees, both managers and their direct reports, found this process rewarding in itself. Those that stuck to it increased both productivity and quality of work life. Appraisal itself became an ongoing process. Formal appraisal meetings were led by direct reports rather than by supervisors. They ended up as summaries of all the informal interactions throughout the appraisal period. The meetings were used mainly to scan the future and reset strategic priorities.

Master Task Six: Pragmatic Leadership

Like excellence, leadership is a familiar concept but hard to define, because it is so complex. Burns's (1978) monumental work, filled with amazing vignettes, is more of a descriptive essay than a theory of leadership. He concedes from the start that leadership is one of the most observed but least understood phenomena on earth.

If managers are to speak meaningfully about leadership, they must start with a discussion of what leadership means and what kind of leadership a particular company needs. It is impossible to discuss a comprehensive approach to business, organizational, and managerial effectiveness without including leadership. The principle is clear:

Master Task Six: Develop leaders at every level of the organization to provide institution-enhancing innovation and change.

Since there are so many different definitions of leadership, it is essential to outline what all of them have in common. This gives us the essence of leadership.

The Essence of Leadership: Performance Beyond the Ordinary

Someone says to you, "Jane and John are real leaders; they consistently deliver ordinary results, they meet targets." A smile comes to your lips because there is an incongruity here. You are amused because you instinctively know that leadership is not about ordinary results. If it is to have meaning, it must refer to those who deliver results beyond the ordinary, either in a single instance—"she handled that merger in a way that exceeded everyone's expectations"—or in some ongoing way—"John's a real leader, he consistently gets the best from his team members." Leadership is in direct contrast to mediocrity.

On the other hand, "results beyond the ordinary" is not the same as "extraordinary" results. If it were, then leadership would be beyond the reach of almost everyone; it would refer only to the heroes and heroines among us. For now, suffice it to say that leadership needs to be rescued from those who would make it mean too much or too little. Everyone in the company needs to know what it means. And whatever it means in the context of a specific company, workers at all levels of the institution must be capable of achieving it. Montgomery Ward, in recasting job descriptions for store managers, made it explicit that the managers were to assume a leadership role. "Results beyond the ordinary"—in terms of strategy implementation, employee commitment to the company's vision, customer service, and people development—were expected. Results beyond the competition. Results beyond last year's. Results beyond what is generally expected in retailing.

The Subtasks of Pragmatic Leadership

The seven subtasks of building a leadership system are outlined as follows. In order to illustrate the subtasks of leadership, some of the cases we have already seen in exploring the first five master tasks will be revisited.

1. Business-Enhancing Change and Buy-In. Make it clear to everyone that leadership is about business-improving change that workers in the institution believe in and make happen. Leadership is not about the traits of the leader or some kind of magical charisma. It is about business-improving change that leads to results beyond the ordinary. Leaders do regular things well or make new things happen. In the case of the chemical company discussed earlier, management realized that many changes were needed to play in the new global petrochemical marketplace. The company needed a new strategy, new joint ventures and strategic partnerships, a new global organization to deliver the strategy, a slimmer and more cost-efficient organization, world-class manufacturing in its plants, a more deeply empowered and involved workforce with a new global mentality, and changes in the company culture to support all the above. The managers were to lead the change and secure buy-in and commitment.

2.   Leadership as a Practical Process. Make sure everyone knows precisely what your company or institution means by leadership. *Develop and promulgate a practical leadership process that everyone can use.* The mass merchandiser turned specialty retailer discussed previously asked its managers to play a critical role in the leadership process it developed, which consisted of the following steps: (1) spotting business-improving ideas from any source, (2) translating these ideas into viable projects, (2) getting buy-in, commitment to, and ownership of these projects by those who could achieve them, (4) creating an organizational climate that supports such innovative projects, and (5) seeing the projects through to conclusion. Obviously, it was not the managers' job to do all this but to see to it that it happened. For instance, one regional manager spotted a good idea in a furniture specialty store — furniture by the room. Furniture and accessories were displayed by the room, and the total package or subpackages were for sale at value prices. Someone at corporate headquarters reworked the concept to fit the company's home furnishings strategy, turning it into a viable project. The president got behind the idea, and he and the vice president of home furnishings sold the idea both to buyers and to the stores. A project champion from corporate and one from the field teamed up to keep the concept on track. The first part of the concept was implemented within six months, and subsequent sales figures proved the viability of the concept.

3.   Leadership as an Interactive Process. Help everyone understand that leadership is a collaborative process that involves leaders and participants in specific situations. While there will always be charismatic leaders who produce results seemingly by the sheer force of their personalities, companies and institutions cannot count on finding

such leaders. The vast majority of institutions need a more democratic approach to leadership. In the case of the chemical company, which had its share of charismatic leaders, it defined
leadership as an interactive process — team-focused leadership,
if you will. Leaders were to be catalysts in this process, doing
some of the work themselves but more often acting as cheerleaders for others. The company encouraged managers to spend
time with their direct reports, tapping into their ideas for improving the company and encouraging them to do the same with
the people they managed.

4. All-Pervasive Leadership. *Recognize that "headship" is not the
same as leadership. Develop leaders at every level of the organization. Recognize and reward everyone who exercises leadership.* In the chemical company case, the business established an employee involvement
program that encouraged everyone to share ideas for making
the business better. In one plant, a technician shared an idea
for improving a catalytic process. The executive vice president
congratulated him on the idea, which would save the company
thousands of dollars. The technician replied, "I knew how to
do this seven years ago, but no one seemed interested." The
vice president realized that leadership could be found everywhere
throughout the organization: executive leadership, managerial
leadership, staff leadership, supervisory leadership, professional-
technical leadership, and operator leadership, that is, leadership on the shop floor as he was now witnessing. Some might
fault the technician for not selling his idea to the company and
therefore completing the leadership process, but at the same time
the culture of the company discouraged ideas from the shop floor.

5. Appropriate Leadership. *Match the right kind of leadership to
each situation.* There are many different ways and many different areas in which leadership can be exercised; that is, there
are many different "brands" of leadership. Some common brands
are strategist, product champion, entrepreneur, crisis manager,
negotiator, public relations expert, quality champion, and so
forth. Precisely which brand is called for depends on the current business needs of the company. One person might do an

extraordinary job in turning a company around, but this does not mean that he or she is the best person to run it over the long haul. One company, in choosing the manager of a new plant, limited his tenure. The company knew that he would be excellent in getting the place up and running — providing a wealth of business-improving ideas himself and getting others to do the same — but not in keeping it going. The company had discovered, sometimes painfully, that it was a mistake to think that a person, because he or she is good in one area, will automatically be good in another. It was unfair to the person and to the company.

6. *Leadership Development. Factor leadership development into all development programs. Train people to think about ways to improve the business. Avoid taking a* trait approach *to leadership.* The specialty retailer needed leadership in implementing strategy, in customer service, and in developing people. While certain champions emerged in these areas, the company needed more leaders everywhere. In developing others, managers were expected to identify those with an extra bit of "spark" and help them move beyond being good contributors to become leaders. The company reviewed and rejected a bid from a consulting firm to train leaders for two reasons. First, the consulting company focused on training people in leadership traits that sounded like they were taken from the Girl Scouts' Oath. The retailer's managers knew that this trait approach would not work. Second, the company believed that it could develop its own formula for leadership development, one that would grow organically from its other development efforts.

create your own desired results

7. *A Learning Organization. Create a learning-organization culture dedicated to constant improvement. Promote practical, business-enhancing learning everywhere in the organization.* In the automaker case discussed, the company wanted to emulate Toyota. During a twenty-year period the Japanese automotive firm had received from its employees some forty million ideas for improving its products aand everything else in the company and had implemented over twenty-eight million of them. A learning or-

learning to re-invent your business regularly

ganization is a company or institution committed to constant improvement. The automaker knew that the vast majority of these improvements would be incremental. But incremental improvements—witness Toyota—can add up to outstanding success and also lay the groundwork for larger breakthroughs. Constant improvement, the automotive concern realized, constituted a philosophy totally different from the "get more and more work from employees" philosophy that had prevailed in its early years.

These subtasks, which contribute to building a leadership system within the company or institution, together with the essential outcome of leadership—performance beyond the ordinary—are illustrated in Figure 5.2.

Leadership: Fostering Innovation and Change

Leaders are contributors who help the company, institution, community, or group move beyond itself, that is, increase its

Figure 5.2. The Subtasks of Pragmatic Leadership.

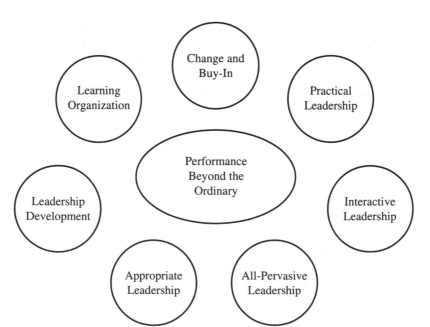

productivity or improve its business-enhancing quality of work life. They do such things as provide new direction, help reconceptualize the management system's mission, identify more effective products, services, or work programs, and discover new resources. Both business leaders and academics have suggested that the essence of leadership is "business-enhancing change."

Here, then, is one results-focused leadership process aimed at improving the system and getting others to contribute to the change process. As suggested earlier, leaders do not do everything in this process by themselves. Rather, they play a critical role in making the process come to life within the institution. There are five steps in this leadership process: (1) coming up with creative business-enhancing ideas, (2) turning these ideas into viable projects and programs, (3) communicating with people and getting them to commit to these projects, (4) creating a supportive climate for these innovative projects, and (5) seeing the projects through to completion.

1. *Business-enhancing ideas.* While good ideas that serve the business are the starting point for this leadership process, this does not mean that the leader is the source of these ideas. Leaders come up with good ideas themselves, recognize them when others present them, and encourage others to think creatively. These may be simple ideas for improving the way a product is made or a service is delivered, or they may be grand visions for the future of the company or institution. Leaders, while realistic, are not tied down to the present. In good times they develop visions of an even better future; in bad times they develop visions of survival even when the odds are bleak.

In the case considered here to illustrate this results-focused leadership process, the administrator of a health care center believed that a total quality management program, judiciously introduced, would go far to help the company revamp its procedures, contain its costs, and improve the quality of care and medical outcomes.

2. *Viable projects and programs.* Leaders are not mere visionaries. With the help of others they translate good ideas or visions into realistic projects and agendas. Sometimes one per-

son will come up with the idea, another with the project or
agenda. The health care center administrator formed a committee to get the TQM program started. In the beginning, she
did not involve doctors. She wanted some successes before asking the medical staff to get on board. Two early projects focused
on nursing staff turnover and admissions waiting time. The administrator was sure that costs for nursing temps could be
reduced. She was also sure that admissions waiting time could
be drastically reduced. Doing something about the former would
also help the morale of nurses; doing something about the latter would improve customer service considerably. She knew that
quick fixes would not work and that systemic solutions would
take time.

   3.   *Communication: generating commitment.* Leaders, whether
personally reserved or outgoing, are good communicators in the
sense that they get their ideas across to others and get them to
rally around projects or agendas. Again, in a results-focused
leadership process, one person may come up with the project
and another may communicate and sell it to others. Furthermore, leaders are not blindly committed to their own projects
and agendas. They offer them to others for constructive critique.
The health care administrator sought the help of certain key
nurses who in turn enlisted the help of one sympathetic doctor
for her first project, reducing nursing staff turnover. They set
themselves up as a task force. A cross-functional team was
formed to tackle the problem of admissions waiting time. Members of these two groups gave some of their own free time to
the projects.

   4.   *A supportive climate.* Leaders create a climate of learning, innovation, and problem solving around their agendas.
Even if the company is not a learning organization, leaders see
to it that a supportive climate of learning surrounds their project
or agenda. They create a ferment around their programs. Their
projects and agendas bring out the creativity of those involved
in developing and implementing them. The agendas stimulate
learning in terms of new options and facilitate problem solving
by moving obstacles out of the way.

   Early on, the admissions group offered a few simple suggestions that reduced the admissions waiting time from three hours to two. This seized the imagination of others, who offered to help the committee with its work. The nursing staff turnover group focused on the key factors that impeded quality of work life in a quasi-public forum that attracted the attention of many. The team members made it clear that this was a nonrecriminatory opportunity for staff to get their complaints out in the open. Good ideas for reducing turnover without raising costs began to flow.

    5.   *Persistence.* Leaders are persistent; they see agendas through to completion. Leaders do not let go; they get things done. In one sense, they do not know the meaning of failure. If they cannot move one way, they will move another. They have setbacks, possibly, but failure, no. Indeed, at the health care center there was some cynicism about both projects; but there is always the "here we go again" group. The administrator and the team members ignored the naysayers. Eventually, the center reduced its cost for nursing temps some 42 percent. Nurses stayed because they found a problem-solving system for dealing with grievances and they saw some doctors buy in to the programs. The results of the admissions project were spectacular; waiting time was reduced from an average of three hours to an average of twenty-one minutes.

Many companies encourage their managers to be leaders, but few describe and install a leadership system that defines leadership for the company and maps out a process for exercising it. The principles just described can be used to develop a leadership formula for any company or institution.

A Summary of the Uses of Model A

Managers can use Model A in various ways. The model is an integrating framework, a practical tool for designing a system or subsystem, a guide for managing a system, an instrument for assessing a system, a cognitive map of a system, and a framework for organizing system interventions. Because it is all of these, it provides managers with a common language for talking about business, organizational, managerial, and leadership issues.

1. *An integrating framework: systems thinking.* The six master tasks of Model A constitute an integrating framework, enabling managers to think systemically about the business, the organization, and management itself. It is a framework for both understanding and acting on the interconnectedness of things.

2. *A practical tool for designing a system or subsystem.* Model A is a kind of generic template that can be used to put a system, unit, or project together "from scratch." At its simplest, it is a checklist that helps managers design systems — units, projects, programs — in an orderly way and prevents them from overlooking critical issues. For instance, for someone wanting to start a restaurant or a retail computer store, Model A provides a design template. Internally, for someone wanting to start a separate training unit within the human resources department, Model A is a design tool.

3. *A practical guide for managing a system.* The six master tasks together with their subtasks (plus any peculiar to a particular company) can be used by managers to create the business-enhancing formulas that make sense for their institution at any given time. Since these tasks are based on the needs of the business, they help managers make value-added decisions.

4. *A primary assessment tool.* A working knowledge of Model A helps the members of an organization discover what is and is not working. Model A can be used as a "radar" device by placing it over a company or one of its units as one would a radar screen. The "red blips" that appear on the screen signify the inconsistencies, the trouble spots, the danger points, and the areas that need attention. The "green blips" signify the opportunities, core competencies, and strengths that need to be leveraged. Model A, then, is the first step, the diagnostic or assessment step, of Model B, the step-by-step process of change.

5. *A cognitive map of the organization.* Model A outlines the "geography" of the business and the organization that is supposed to serve it. In the case of managerial interventions, it makes the point of entry into the system visually clear. It also makes it quite clear that such interventions are systemic. For instance, the realignment of the marketing plan can set off a wave of changes. Model A helps a manager keep track of them.

6.   *A framework for organizing system interventions.* Model A can help identify the specific business and organizational development technologies that are needed to handle the problems of a company or institution. For instance, if relationships and communication are poor within a specific team, team building may be called for. On the other hand, business problems such as the drying up of markets will not be solved by team building. Model A, since it is a broad-band model of design and facilitation, helps prevent administrators, directors, managers, consultants, and other change agents from using pet but inappropriate technologies in addressing system problems.

7.   *A common language for talking about systems.* A shared understanding of Model A helps all those involved in a company — executives, managers, supervisors, professionals, operators, and consultants — speak a common language and therefore cooperate more effectively in both running the system and assessing the need for change. For instance, the ability to discuss business versus organizational factors can help people identify blind spots that make them overemphasize organization processes at the expense of business outcomes.

SIX

Managing the Shadow Side
of the Organization

Although it would seem logical to move from Model A to Model B, Model C, which deals with the arational or shadow side dimensions of companies and institutions, is discussed in this chapter. The reason is both to give depth or a third-dimensional perspective to Model A and to prepare the way for the shadow side of Model B. Mastering Models A and B — designing, running, and changing a system — helps make managers smart. Integrating Model C into all managerial thinking and acting can help make managers wise.

Understanding the shadow side of an organization can help managers avoid two polar pitfalls — naïveté and cynicism. Concepts found in Model C permeate Models A and B. Effective managers tend to be savvy and street-smart, not naïve. They know what is going on in their organization. They are not blindsided by organizational politics. They know that management is the art of the possible, that decisions, even good decisions, often "emerge" rather than get handed down by edict. If they avoid naïveté, they also avoid cynicism. The cynic is someone who has given up but who has not shut up. Good managers know how to keep cynics from polluting the atmosphere; they best know how to get them to add value to the enterprise. Between naïveté on the one hand and cynicism on the other lies

88

realism. Model C gets the master tasks and subtasks of Model A and the challenges of Model B out of the textbooks and into the realities of the street, as it were. The premise for Model C is that managers need to know what is going on and be able to do something about it.

Consider this situation. Susan knew that her boss, John, was an alcoholic. John was one of a group of six people who had started the company. So he was there to stay. Because of his sporadic drinking, which no one discussed openly, he had become marginal to the company's major decision-making process. When he was sober, he could be trusted completely and added a great deal of value to the company. When he was drinking, his decisions were flawed. Susan was both savvy and skilled. She gained John's trust. When it was clear to her that John was drinking, she monitored his decisions more carefully. She convinced him to defer some decisions and modify others.

The situation was not perfect. Ultimately, John needed to do something about his alcoholism; in the meantime, Susan handled the situation in the best way possible.

Model C provides no magic. It deals with the kind of realities that Susan faced and the choices managers can make to handle them.

An Advanced Organizer: What Chapter Six Is About

- *What Is the Shadow Side?* The shadow side refers to realities that often disrupt, and sometimes benefit, the business but are not dealt with in the formal settings of the organization. The five aspects of the shadow side are presented throughout the rest of the chapter.
- *Business and Organizational Messiness: The Shadow Side of Model A.* Repeated mistakes in strategy, operations, structure, human resource management, choice and development of managers, and leadership point to realities "in the shadows" that the company is not coming to grips with.
- *The Shadow Side of People.* Knowing how to identify and manage individuals' idiosyncrasies can add great value to the company.

- *The Shadow Side of the Social System.* The ways in which people pursue social needs in the workplace can add value or cost to the business. Being able to manage diversity is becoming a necessity.
- *The Shadow Side of Organizational Politics.* Positive politics, the politics of negotiated agendas that serve the business, can add great value; negative politics, the politics of self-interest, are often both covert and costly.
- *Culture: "The Way We Do Things Here."* A company's culture is considered the largest and most controlling of the systems because it dictates norms for everything else. Norms of the covert culture can stymie everything; a culture that serves the business can liberate people's energies.

Model C, insofar as it identifies realities that affect the business, identifies "the needs of the business," just as Model A does. Insofar as it provides awareness of shadow side realities and suggests methods and skills for coping with them, Model C helps managers deal with the real world. Both awareness ("look at what's going on") and skills ("I think I know how to handle this") are needed to manage shadow side realities.

What Is the Shadow Side?

Many people talk about the limitations of rational models in designing, managing, and changing organizations. To be sure, the best managers have always, at least at a gut level, sensed these limitations and have acted accordingly. Model C is not an attack on rationality. Individual managers can hurt the business by being too rational or by not being rational enough. The manager who does everything by the letter of the law can cause a great deal of damage. Often enough, when workers, say, air traffic controllers, want to express their displeasure to management, they "work to rule." Working to rule can soon bring an institution to its knees. This tells us something about the "rationality" of the rules in the first place. On the other hand, managers who consistently rely on intuition rather than analysis, or their hearts rather than their heads, to make decisions may soon have nothing to manage.

Definition of the Shadow Side

The "shadow side" does not necessarily mean the irrational. Here is my definition of what makes up the shadow side:

The shadow side of a company or institution includes the factors that affect, either positively or negatively, organizational productivity and quality of work life in substantive and systematic ways but are not found on organizational charts or in organizational manuals and are not discussed in the formal or official forums of the institution.

When is the last time an official meeting of your company or institution was dedicated to a discussion of internal politics? When did an examination of company cliques and how they help or hurt the business last make the agenda? Has there ever been a discussion on the use of intuition in decision making? What about the covert arrangements of the "informal organization" that are in place, some of them helping, some hindering productivity and quality of work life? Certainly these things get discussed. Sometimes those who work in a company spend a great deal of time discussing some of them, such as organizational politics. For obvious reasons, however, shadow side issues do not make their way to the official forums of companies.

Understanding and Dealing with the Arational

Understanding and dealing with the arational in organizations is important because managers spend a great deal of time and energy dealing with shadow side realities. How much time and energy is consumed in dealing with a difficult employee? How much more energy is needed to manage a group that is guarding its turf to the detriment of the business? What is a manager to do about a covert organizational arrangement that is limiting the effectiveness of the business? Indeed, what is a manager to do about a covert organizational arrangement that violates some of the company's rules but is adding value to the business? What if the assumptions, beliefs, values, and norms of the prevailing culture do not support a proposed new strategy? When managers are given an opportunity to name shadow side realities that consume a great deal of time and energy, the floodgates are opened. They say that in times of crisis over 80 percent of their time and energy is consumed with the arationalities of the system. Even in "normal" times, many claim, over half their energy is taken up by these concerns. Percentages are not important; adding value by managing the shadow side is.

Negative and Positive Forms of Arationality

The term *arational* need not have the negative connotations that the term *irrational* does. If a manager were to shoot a staff member because of his or her incompetence, that would be irrational. However, when a manager retains a staff member even though he or she has, over a considerable period of time, proved to be less than competent, is the manager being irrational or rather involved in one of the more common system-limiting arationalities of organizational life? Furthermore, *arational* does not imply that someone is wrong or at fault. For instance, that the director of a correctional facility and her assistant enter an expressed or implied contract on the division of labor between them and then both, in different ways, fail to live up to some minor provisions of the contract does not necessarily argue for ill will.

Failure to live up to contracts in minor ways is one of the normal arationalities of life. The problem is that these minor deviations add up and often lead to some kind of crisis, especially when the parties of the contract fail to talk about the deviations they notice and often resent. A strictly rational view of contracts would demand that each party consistently live up to the letter of the contract. In practice, this strictly rational approach to contracts does not prevail. Witness marriage. Certainly I am not advocating a sloppy or cynical approach to contracts. It would be irrational or unethical for parties to enter into a contract the substance of which they have no intention of honoring. But contracts are human instruments permeated by human strength and human frailty.

The shadow side of an organization does not necessarily refer to a *dark side* in the negative sense of that term. Emotions by definition are arational, but this does not make them irrational or unreasonable. In fact, it is quite reasonable for people to feel and express emotions even in organizational settings. Emotions add depth and color to human interactions. A manager who is both enthusiastic and stimulates enthusiasm among the members of her team is involved in a system-enhancing use of emotion. Inappropriate and irresponsible expressions of emotion are another matter. If a supervisor constantly uses anger as a way of exercising control over the members of the project team, then his use of emotion becomes irrational or unreasonable.

Emotion is often a double-edged sword. Entrepreneurs are usually enthusiastic about their ventures, and their enthusiasm provides a great deal of drive. But this same enthusiasm can prevent them from seeing dangers and pitfalls until it is too late. For instance, the enthusiasm of an entrepreneur buying an existing business can easily prevent him or her from seeing through some of the seller's exaggerations, calculating the possibility of a recession, foreseeing enormous hikes in the advertising rates of the local newspaper, sensing a narrowing market for the business, or factoring in competition from nationwide chains.

The statement "My head tells me no, but my heart says yes; I'll follow my heart" is probably arational rather than irrational. It is an emotional form of intuition. Much individual behavior is arational rather than irrational. An expectation that everyone will always follow the rational path is in itself irrational. From another perspective, the rational is what might be expected in the world if everyone were to follow reason all the time. The arational refers to deviations from reason, which are common among human beings.

There are many system-enhancing forms of the arational — creativity of various sorts, the judicious use of intuition in making decisions, and many of the "arrangements" and "common conspiracies" found in the informal organization — to name but a few. Many forms of the arational can be, in different circumstances or from different points of view, either system enhancing or system limiting. For instance, the use of intuition in decision making can lead to amazing creativity or to disaster. Yet, in a world as complex as ours, the use of some intuition in making decisions is inescapable.

Shadow Side Categories

Businesses obviously do not proceed with the kind of efficiency intimated by Model A. Model A presents principles that each company, institution, or unit has to turn into its own ever-changing formulas. Execution of the methods of Model A is never perfect and never will be, despite today's push toward constant improvement and total quality. Companies and institutions are filled with imperfect people, often delightfully imperfect, but still imperfect.

Every system casts a shadow because there is a "shadow" or arational side to our humanity. Effective managers understand and learn how to manage the shadow side of the institution even though they may not name it as such or do so with full consciousness. The five shadow side areas considered in Model C are as follows.

1. Various forms of business, organizational, and managerial messiness
2. Individual problems and idiosyncracies
3. The organization as a social sysem and all the diversity a social system entails
4. The organization as a political system and the continual struggle for scarce resources
5. Organizational culture, the largest and most controlling organizational system

Business and Organizational Messiness: The Shadow Side of Model A

Model A, unlike models governed by the laws of the physical sciences, depends on human intervention and is therefore prone to human fads and foibles. To get a feeling for the way shadow side realities permeate the day-to-day operations of any given company or institution, I review here two forms of arationality: the loosely coupled nature of most enterprises and the prevalence of the informal system.

The Loosely Coupled Nature of Most Enterprises

If the world were magic, then companies and institutions would consistently operate the way they are depicted in business plans and on organizational charts. In business plans sources of capital are found to develop the business, the level of debt needed to serve the business is stabilized, strategy drives operations, the organization serves the business, and organizational units such as design, engineering, and manufacturing work seamlessly together. Inputs are transformed, almost effortlessly, into outputs that lead to our three desired outcomes: satisfied customers, committed and productive employees, and good financial returns. And all of this is coordinated, facilitated, and controlled by a cadre of well-functioning managers, many of whom are leaders. On paper, then, most enterprises seem to be relatively tightly knit.

But alas it is not so. What is tightly knit on paper is often loosely coupled in fact. Strategy is often a document that sits in someone's drawer or a publicized plan that drives operations and organizational programs and tasks only to a degree. The organization serves the vested interests of the workforce just as much as it serves the business. Human resource management systems are either nonexistent or poorly formulated and add little value to the business. The point is that things that have parts are often put together poorly and, once put together, tend to fall apart. This applies to companies and institutions just as much as it applies to machinery. The complexity of even small enterprises courts shadow side messiness.

One organization I worked with had a "strategic planning" unit located in the human resources department. When I asked them what happened to the analyses they kept on making, they said that they sent them "upstairs." When I asked what impact their reports had, the answer was almost predictable: "Very little, as far as we can see." Here was an organizational unit that added practically no value, and those working in the unit knew it. This part of the organization was certainly loosely coupled with the business, but it kept doing its work until a severe cost-cutting push made it an easy target.

Wise managers are not misled by what is written on paper or depicted on charts. Understanding the loosely coupled nature of their enterprises, they know when to move into maintenance-and-repair mode just as well as they know when to move into creation-and-innovation mode. Frequently, when new CEOs are brought in from outside, they do amazingly well, at least for the first few years. One CEO said to me, "It's amazing how much money you can make by stopping doing the wrong things." Possessing the unobstructed vision of the outsider, they see clearly what is loosely coupled and what is falling apart. Unencumbered by political ties, they can clean the organization up and get a lot of good press for doing so.

One new CEO, fully supported by the board, came into a company, took one look around, immediately saw the ways in which the moribund company had become loosely coupled, closed or sold four of the company's divisions, set a new strategy, made it clear to everyone that the new strategy would drive the business, installed single-minded presidents in the still viable divisions, trimmed the fat, established new working charters with suppliers and customers, and through the dint of hard work watched the company revive. A number of years later he was complaining about the lack of both strategic and operational synergy among the now viable divisions, the ways in which new kingdoms had been created, and the fact that the set of values he had espoused and that had driven the turnaround had not penetrated very deeply into the divisions. Prevention, he realized, was much more difficult than cleanup, as it required a higher-order wisdom. Seeing this aspect of the company's shadow side was quite helpful. The CEO could do something about these realities before they took up permanent residence and once again dragged the company down.

The Prevalence of the Informal System

Much of Model A is a description of the *formal system,* that is, the set of arrangements that is publicly and officially endorsed by the system. But there is also an *informal system:*

The informal system *refers to the set of arrangements that actually exists within the system but does not have official public endorsement. The arrangements often contravene or take precedence over formal rules, regulations, and policies.*

Managing the informal system is not usually part of a manager's job description. But perhaps it should be, because the arrangements conducted under the informal system can either enhance or limit the productivity of the organization. For instance, a tenured professor at a private university was head of one of the departments in the school of education. He supposedly delegated a great deal of his responsibility to faculty members in his department. He also "did a lot of work at home." A dabbler in the financial markets, he had also developed an informal investment counseling business. A new dean, when he arrived at the university, discovered that there were a number of such arrangements in place. The arrangements added no value to the school. Other covert arrangements, however, were quite different. One faculty member consulted a great deal with public high schools and published her findings. As a result of her work, she brought a wealth of examples to the classroom and arranged internships in various schools for her students. In doing all of this, however, she broke the official rule for the amount of time professors were allowed to spend on paid consulting. Yet this set of arrangements added a great deal of value to the school.

Given human ingenuity, there will always be sets of informal arrangements. Managing the informal system starts with knowing what the informal arrangements are and then determining whether they are business-enhancing or business-limiting. It is usually not a question of eliminating all arrangements that violate the rules. Nor is it simply a case of ferreting out those that do not add value and turning a blind eye to those that do. In the case just mentioned, the dean eventually replaced the over-delegating department head with a new one who would supervise the deposed professor more closely. Given the tenure system at the university, there was little chance of firing the professor. Early retirement was the most that could be hoped for. The dean also eventually talked to the teacher who was doing

the consulting. In a very circumspect way he intimated that
professional envy might be a problem. The professor cut back
a bit on her consulting and took pains to let her colleagues in
the university and the administration know how her accomplishments added value to the school of education. While neither so-
lution was perfect, both were improvements.

In dealing with the shadow side, consciousness-raising
comes first; forewarned is forearmed. Managers who work from
a shared model of management based on the needs of the business (that is, from some kind of Model A) have a head start
in managing both the loosely coupled nature of most enterprises
and the arrangements of the informal system. Since they have
a relatively clear idea of how to add value to the business, they
can quickly become aware of the common mistakes, games, and
glitches that prevent adding value. They are also aware of
shadow side issues. For instance, when it comes to structure,
they instinctively ask themselves certain critical questions. How
have the structures been altered? How do the alterations make
the business better? How do they serve self-interest and political agendas? How entrenched are the alterations? If the informal structures are challenged, what benefits will be reaped?
What is the cost-benefit ratio of challenging and changing them
now? Similar questions can be formulated for each Model A task.

The Shadow Side of People

A great deal of the arationality of companies, institutions, and
communities stems from the complexity, idiosyncrasies, and un-
predictability of the individual members of these systems. The
complexity of human beings is both charming and infuriating.
Individuals in positions of responsibility (such as managers,
teachers, parents, ministers, judges, doctors, law enforcement
officers) who are wise know "what is in men and women." Without becoming cynical, they are seldom surprised by eruptions
of shadow side behavior. Taking an organic rather than a mech-
anistic view of systems, they make allowances for such things
as individual differences, emotionality, defensiveness, and the

like. They realize that even in totalitarian systems individuals exercise their freedom in a variety of unpredictable ways, and they are not surprised even when individuals seem to use their freedom against themselves. On one hand, encounters with what is best in people encourage intelligent individuals without making them overly optimistic about human nature; on the other hand, encounters with human venality do not discourage them or erode their basic optimism. They take people where they are instead of where they wish they were. They also know that people can be better than they are and thus constantly look at both themselves and others from a development perspective. Not only are they into problem solving and innovation, they also factor shadow side realities into these processes.

Consider this case. Gregory was the chief financial officer for a private residential prep school located in the northeastern United States but with roots in England. Thinking that he was the brightest person on staff, he decided to extend his mandate. He involved himself in almost every aspect of the school's functioning, from curriculum to dining hall menu. He had excellent financial skills and used them to add value to the school, but his interpersonal style and his need to have a say in just about everything turned people off. He did not seem to notice this. For instance, although he did a good job leading a fundraising effort—the goal was substantially exceeded—he annoyed parents and alumni in the process. Some felt that money had been extorted from them. This did not bode well for further fundraising campaigns.

The director of the school, from Britain himself, did not know what to do with him. He felt that the school did depend, perhaps too much, on his financial skills, but he also knew full well that most staff members resented Gregory's heavy-handed ways. In his dealings with the director, Gregory was alternately so ingratiating and so aggressive that it left the former almost paralyzed. That a recession had hit the Northeast quite hard and that enrollments were down added to his reluctance to face up to Gregory.

He waited too long. Both his deputy and the headmaster of the school announced at the end of the term that they were leaving and had already accepted positions for the next school year. They both said that the "climate" was too difficult to work in. (Gregory, true to form, had suggestions for their replacements before the week was out.) No one, including the director, had ever challenged Gregory's style. He had never been discussed in any public forum (for instance, with the members of the school board), even though staff members talked and joked about him frequently. Though the issues were "public," it was a shadow side case indeed.

Defensive Postures in the Workplace

When reality becomes too intrusive, people develop strategies for warding it off. For instance, early in life most of us become fairly adept at face-saving excuse making. Face-saving behavior, as Goffman (1967) illustrates so well, is not a form of behavior relegated to Middle Eastern or Far Eastern societies. It is alive and well in the West as well. People want their performance reviewed favorably, whether these reviews come from self or others. Failures and performance that fall short of some standard must be explained away. "Excuses," according to Snyder, Higgins, and Stucky (1983), "are explanations or actions that lessen the negative implications of an actor's performance, thereby maintaining a positive image for oneself and others" (p. 45). Since excuse making is rewarded — it often gets people off the hook — it is used often. In fact, it can become so instinctive and habitual that individuals are not even aware of their excuse-making behavior.

Chris Argyris has done extensive research on system-limiting defensiveness in the workplace. Managers do not always say what they really mean, though they tend to deny this when challenged. Nor do they routinely test the beliefs and assumptions they hold about the business, the organization, or management practices. They are not really as open as they often pretend to be. Some do not even realize what they are doing. Their communication skills, aimed at avoiding conflict in the workplace, produce an unintended by-product — mixed messages and the failure to make timely business decisions. Argyris defines defensive routines as "any action or policy designed to avoid surprise, embarrassment, or threat" (1986, p. 75), that is, outcomes that have negatively valenced emotions associated with them. These routines are not just part of the communication style of individual managers; they become part of the organization's covert culture. How they limit the system's effectiveness is usually not seen until some disaster occurs.

Skills Needed to Manage the Shadow Side of People

It is impossible to outline in a short space the full range of skills managers need to deal with shadow side realities. Therefore, a brief focus on some of the skills needed to manage the shadow side of individuals will give the "flavor" of the kinds of skills needed. Again, the arationality of individuals is not the same as irrationality, and many forms of arationality give breadth, depth, and color to life. There are a number of ways of managing workplace arationality without becoming an amateur psychologist. They all require certain basic skills.

Awareness. Heightened awareness, what we might call a "working psychology" of people, is the starting point for managing all forms of the shadow side of individuals. This includes a working knowledge of the common forms of arationality exhibited by human beings. We are not talking about neurotic or psychotic behavior here, except to say that supervisors should know when they are facing problems with a worker that are beyond their professional ability to handle from both a legal and a psychological point of view. Managers will not move beyond system-limiting defensive routines unless they first become aware of these routines. Therefore, a training program in human behavior in the workplace would seem to be the starting point for managers and supervisors. Outlining common system-limiting foibles in the workplace would be part of this program.

In the prep school case in the previous section, the director hired a very savvy deputy, Andrew, a former priest who had spent a number of years in one of his order's residential schools. In the weeks running up to the opening of school, Andrew quickly took in the entire drama. He watched Gregory interact with his colleagues. For Andrew, Gregory's power games were clear—intimidation, cajoling, switching sides. He wondered why the others put up with them.

Understanding Human Motivation. Since most human actions are subject to the laws of human behavior in terms of incentives, rewards, and punishment, a basic understanding of these laws would be most useful. If people consistently avoid work or do a poor job, the odds are that there are more incentives for not working or for doing a slipshod job than the opposite. This is usually a managerial rather than a worker problem.

Andrew realized that the director, even though he had authority on his side, thought that he was no match for Gregory. It was clear that he did not want to engage Gregory because he thought he would lose and, even more important, the school would lose. These fears were strong motivators. It was also clear to Andrew why Gregory played the game—he felt the exercise of power rewarding and he never lost. These were also powerful motivators.

Opportunity Development Versus Problem Solving. Some managers focus on problems rather than opportunities. Sometimes this is warranted. Often enough, however, there would be fewer problems if there were a greater emphasis on pursuing opportunities. A versatile opportunity developer and problem solver is not daunted by the arationality of the people with whom he or she interacts. The shadow side is part of the challenge.

Andrew flipped the Gregory problem to the other side, the opportunity angle. He thought that Gregory could be managed in a way that would enable everyone to win—the school, the students, the director, the parents, and even Gregory. The school could benefit from Gregory's considerable talents, but in a much more focused way. The director could develop a bit of courage. Gregory could learn that his present style was ultimately self-defeating and that another, more positive style might be more realistic and even, in the longer term, more rewarding.

Communication Skills. Managers can develop communication and counseling skills that can greatly facilitate their interactions with one another (see Egan, 1990a, 1990b). The following skills are most useful for managers and leaders:

- *Listening skills.* The ability to listen to both verbal and nonverbal messages without distorting them through personal, system, or cultural filters is essential. This "total listening" includes contextual listening, or "listening" to a person's behavior as embedded in and influenced by the workplace and other social settings of the person's life, rather than as isolated conduct occurring in a vacuum. Few managers listen very well. How many good ideas go unheeded because of failure to listen? How many opportunities to add value are lost?

Andrew watched and "listened to" the entire story. He heard the director's struggle. He listened closely to what Gregory had to say and to the hidden meaning behind the messages. For instance, when Gregory said, "I have an idea," lurking in the background was the more sinister "This is what you must do if you don't want to be stupid." Andrew kept his listening unbiased; it was important to understand just what was going on.

- *Listening-based responses.* The ability to communicate to another person that you have, to the best of your ability, understood what he or she has had to say from his or her viewpoint is a fundamental communication skill. It is the beginning of dialogue. Research shows that such empathic response is not common in human transactions; people tend to listen and respond selectively. Empathy is a skill that helps build relationships and gather the kind of information that is useful in managing human transactions.

People felt comfortable around Andrew. They thought he understood because of the way he responded to them. He not only listened to people's ideas, but his responses indicated that he had got to the core of their messages. Gregory did not know what to think. Like the others, he liked being understood, but he knew that Andrew was no fool. His very communication skills had a kind of power to them.

- *Challenging skills.* Challenging means inviting others to explore assumptions, beliefs, values, attitudes, norms, and behaviors that may be hindering individuals or the system. There are many different forms of challenging, including the kinds of ongoing feedback, both confirmatory and corrective, that are essential for a performance system worthy of the name (Egan, 1990a). Confirmatory feedback is a challenge to keep to high standards; corrective feedback is a challenge to do better. Challenging, including feedback, works best when it is not a personal attack and does not back the other person into a corner. Effective challengers know how to challenge themselves and how to invite others to do the same. They also challenge people more on their unused strengths than on their weaknesses. This kind of challenge is not common among managers.

Andrew quickly gained the confidence of the director. He pointed out to him that his failure to face up to Gregory was limiting the effectiveness of the school, something that the director already knew deep in his heart. While the director's failure to act stemmed from his British sensibility of propriety, it was also a failure in courage. Andrew focused on the director's communication style, not his lack of courage: "I know that challenging people is not your style, but. . . . " He helped the director review the kinds of messages he had to deliver to Gregory and how he might do so. These dialogues revealed a strength in the director that had not been apparent before—not even to the director.

- *Innovation-focused dialogue.* If opportunity development rather than mere problem solving is a managerial priority, then innovation-focused dialogue among managers and between managers and their reports is essential. Some problems need to be transcended rather than solved or even managed. If a company is losing market share to a competitor, "solving" the problem means winning back market share. An opportunity-development approach suggests moving to a higher plane—discovering new markets, finding niches, changing the product mix, and the like. The issue is not necessarily regaining market share but remaining profitable. Managers often do not consistently engage in innovation-focused dialogue with one another and with their reports.

Andrew and the director asked themselves, "If this problem were turned into an opportunity, what would it look like?" One answer: there would be a management team running the school, consisting of the director, the deputy, the headmaster, and the chief financial officer. This group would operate under a charter. Even though the director would have veto power, he would use it only if absolutely necessary. Every member of the team would be a contributor, but each would be expected to be a team player. The school could not operate without teamwork. This upbeat scenario served as the basis of the director's dialogue with Gregory.

• *Negotiation skills.* The best managers, realizing that there are many different ways to approach business and organizational issues and problems, learn how to balance different points of view to achieve both business outcomes and quality of work life. While maintaining their principles, they avoid both slovenly compromise and belligerent and unproductive adherence to positions. They dig below positions and help parties in conflict discover common interests. They instinctively think win-win solutions and pursue them in dialogues with relevant stakeholders. Negotiation skills are at the heart of their problem-solving abilities. Managers with good human relations skills can add a great deal of value.

The director confronted Gregory by outlining the needs of the school and what kind of management team was needed to meet these needs. He told him flatly that he preferred to have him on the team, but as a full team member. This would mean an end to the unilateral decisions he was used to taking, but it would also legitimize his best contributions. After a couple of discussions with Gregory, who was smart enough to see the handwriting on the wall, the director convened the first executive management committee meeting to spell out the role of each member and to establish a charter for working together.

Although communication skills are basic to effective management, few managers are proficient in them. One recent study showed that line chiefs at a large farm and industrial equipment company spent over 25 percent of their time on personality clashes. Another study showed that managers in general spend about 20 percent of their time handling conflicts. Therefore, skills like these are not mere amenities. They are essential for dealing effectively with just about every kind of shadow side issue outlined here.

The Shadow Side of the Social System

If there is more than one person in the company, then there is a social system. The social system refers to the society of people in a company, institution, or any specific function or unit and the social interactions among the society's members. In one sense, then, an organization is a social matrix within which people meet their social needs. For instance, in the United States many older people return to work not just because they feel a bit squeezed financially but also because they are looking for a fuller social life. The natural social interactions of the workplace are just the ticket. The sociology of the system encompasses such things as social structure, social diversity, social mores, social cohesion, and fad and fashion. *Information sharing* is a business term; *rumor* is a social system term. Both deal with communication but in far different ways. *Work team* is a business term; *clique* is a social system term. Work teams are routinely discussed in the public forums of an institution. Cliques are not. Since social phenomena affect the business, understanding and managing social issues are critical management skills.

Sociotechnical Systems

Like the "arrangements" discussed earlier, friendships, social groupings, and unplanned interactions within and among these are part of the "informal organization." Like other shadow side dimensions, these groupings do not exist on the formal organizational chart. In the 1920s and 1930s studies done at the Hawthorne Plant of Western Electric Company in Chicago demonstrated the importance of social needs in the workplace. The way workers go about satisfying social needs can either enhance or limit workplace productivity. Companies have always struggled with the "human side" of the workplace, some successfully, some quite unsuccessfully.

Companies and institutions are *sociotechnical systems,* in which workers both individually and collectively use and interact with the technology of the business — computers, coal-mining equipment, trucks, laboratory procedures, or what have you. Sociotechnical experts help companies find the best fit between individuals, social systems, and the technology or work programs of the system. The ideal, of course, is satisfying legitimate social needs in such a way as to increase rather than limit productivity. Since social needs are so diverse and since much of social interaction is hidden from view, integrating social needs and workplace demands will always be a challenge.

Cliques

Cliques or subgroups are part of most institutional social systems. Consider the following example. I was talking to a glum-looking senior manager in an international development institution. When asked what was wrong, he replied that he was having trouble with one of his subordinates. When I heard the story — the manager's story, of course — about the subordinate, I suggested that he fire her. He replied that he could not do that. Taking a rational approach, I pointed out to him that current institution rules, regulations, and policies certainly allowed him to fire her, with some room to spare. "You don't understand," he said, "there are two reasons why I can't fire her, and you haven't touched on either." He went on to explain that the institution had recently become very touchy about women's issues. After all, his institution had been a key participant in the UN-sponsored "decade of the woman," which was just coming to an end. In sum, he was saying that the institution as a society was becoming more concerned about the place of women both among its own employment ranks and in the world. Therefore, firing a woman, even one who clearly presented difficulties, was not easy in the current social climate.

"More important," he continued, "she's a member of a particular nationality." He then explained that he had to do a

lot of work with a director who was also a member of that nationality. "If I were to fire her," he said, "this could well sour
my relationship with him, though he would never admit it. I
need him as an ally over the next year or so to make sure that
two projects move forward. I can't afford to take the risk." He
ended by saying, "I'll have to find ways of walling her off so
that she does not cause any harm. It's not my biggest problem.
I'm just very annoyed with her today."

In some institutions, learning the ropes of the social system, including how to deal with cliques, is a matter of life and
death. One need not be in a reformatory or a penitentiary for
long before the social politics of the place becomes a stark and
even terrifying reality. The social politics of systems and their
accompanying rules of power, pecking order, subgroups, and
so on are not written down and posted. Rather they are acted
out. In a penitentiary, not to know the informal roles of the social system can put the life of a convict in jeopardy. To be una-
ware of the social realities in the workplace may not be life threatening, but it can certainly be career threatening. Managing
social realities, to the degree that this is possible, can add value
to the business and at the same time contribute to the quality
of work life.

Managing the Social System

Given the increasing diversity of the workforce, the tendency
to form social groups based on these diversities is strong and
natural. These groups provide a sense of belonging, identity,
and security. Such groups can either enhance or hinder the business. To the degree that they satisfy legitimate social needs and
encourage teamwork, they add value. To the degree that they
pursue self-interest that is opposed to the common good of the
institution, they add cost of one kind or another.

Since "managing diversity" in the workplace is such a
widely discussed topic currently, what was once in the shadows
has moved partially into the light. But not completely. Managing diversity is highly political, and the politics of diversity is
still in the shadows. Furthermore, there is a covert social sys-

tem within all subgroups. Finally, differences in ethnicity, gender, nationality, sexual orientation, and religion often overlie less obtrusive forms of social differences already embedded in companies and institutions. For instance, societies, including companies, often have "social ladders." Some people are not even on the ladder, and those who are range from low to high. In some companies, marketing staff may enjoy higher status than those in manufacturing. Workers in the human resources department may be much more marginal, approaching the pariah state in some companies. In other companies the financial hotshots may constitute the social elite. In others, salaried workers may constitute a privileged class, with hourly workers more marginal.

There are marginal members in all societies. The society of any given company or institution will never be completely integrated. However, most companies today cannot afford marginality; they need teamwork. If, say, people in marketing or R&D view their colleagues in manufacturing as lower on the totem pole, then customer service might suffer. High-quality customer service is achieved only through teamwork.

All institutions have covert or informal social rules. Sometimes they are humorous. One bank vice president said that she was not sure what someone had to do to become an officer of the bank, but she knew that anyone who wore polyester clothes never would! (That was obviously in the days before researchers found ways of making polyester look and feel like wool or linen.) Learning how to live within the social system, even if you do not like its rules, is something everyone has to come to grips with. Expecting all the rules to be logical and reasonable is — in light of the arationality of social systems — unreasonable in itself.

Since social differences are not going away, managers are left with the task of understanding and managing the social system with both human compassion and business acumen. Somehow managers need to learn how to do this without becoming applied sociologists, just as they need to learn how to supervise individuals without becoming amateur psychologists. Social sensitivity and common sense go a long way, but since one company will differ greatly from another in terms of its social realities, there is no simple formula for managing the system. Once more, awareness is essential. Even if the workforce looks relatively homogeneous on the surface, hidden social phenomena may be affecting the business.

In one company some of the employees complained that the company made too big a deal of Saint Patrick's Day. Before the workforce had become so diverse, everyone joined in and became "Irish" on March 17. Instead of banning Saint Patrick's Day celebrations, the company encouraged other social groups to celebrate their days. And so, Latino Day and Black Pride Day were established. After all, there were enough days in the year to accommodate all groups. In fact, the more the merrier. These celebrations added a bit of interest and zest to the place. In the World Bank, in which more than one hundred nationalities are represented, celebrations of diversity are common. Art exhibits, lectures, and ethnic foods in the cafeteria add interest.

The problem-solving and communication skills mentioned earlier are essential tools for managing the shadow side of social systems. Perhaps *managing* is the wrong word. It makes it sound as if shadow side realities were no different from other business realities such as strategy and operations. The term *awareness* refers to the manager's ability to take a three-dimensional look at the workplace. With respect to the social system, the third dimension refers to the interactions among individuals and among groups. Sensitivity to the dynamics of these interactions can make a difference.

In an earlier example, a hospital administrator did not immediately include doctors in setting up a total quality management process, not because doctors were not critical players but because of the social sensitivities between doctors and other groups in the hospital. Later on this same administrator got doctors who had volunteered for start-up committees to act as facilitators of doctor groups. It was not that the doctors were opposed to the total quality management efforts, but rather the approach had to be one that respected the social realities of the system. Pretending that these social realities were useless and that a totally democratic TQM process was just what was needed would have been naïve. To assume that doctors were not interested in improving both patient care and medical outcomes would have been cynical. The administrator dealt realistically with the social realities of the system.

The Shadow Side of Organizational Politics

While some systems are less political than others, they all have some kind of politics. This includes large conglomerates such as General Motors, institutions such as correctional facilities, and community systems such as churches and families.

The Essence of Politics in Systems

Most of us are familiar with the world of organizational politics. It is a gold mine of arationality. Politics deals with such phenomena as interest groups, coalitions, power, influence, conflict, and negotiation around vested interests. In fact, the essence of organizational politics can be defined thus.

The essence of politics is competition for power, position, turf, prevailing ideology, and resources that are or are perceived to be scarce.

This is not to suggest that vying, debating, and contending in and of themselves are bad. Modulated contention and debate are essential for an institution's vitality. But some kinds of contention add value while others add cost.

Resources. If resources are not scarce, there is no reason to vie for them. If there is an abundance of entry-level jobs in a company, there is little need for political jockeying to secure one. However, if unemployment is high, then the politics of recruitment can be virulent. Management positions are scarce commodities, and in many companies, because of restructuring and downsizing, they are getting even more scarce. In some companies competition for managerial positions is ruthless. Since most institutions still have some kind of pyramid structure, higher positions are even more scarce. Therefore, succession planning is often one of the more politicized human resource practices.

There are many other scarce resources: space, time, titles,

and, of course, money. The jockeying that goes on at budget time is another common example of vying for scarce resources. In an era of cost containment, money for raises and projects, already scarce, has become even more scarce and therefore even more politicized.

Ideology. Ideologies — beliefs, values, and norms insofar as they affect ways of approaching the business and the organization — abound in most companies. There are many different ways things can be done in companies and institutions — different approaches to formulating strategy; different strategies; different priorities among such things as quality, customer service, and cost containment and the ways of promoting them; different ways of structuring work; different packages of authority and responsibility for different jobs; different kinds of human resource management systems; different approaches to performance management and appraisal — different ways to do everything outlined in Model A. But, since ideologies tend to compete with one another, not all can prevail. If one vision of the best direction for a company is to prevail, then a competing one cannot. A company cannot be driven by competing visions. Decisions need to be made, and ideology drives decisions. Those who espouse the prevailing ideology run the show.

Turf. Turf is about protecting the territory and resources a group already has. Turf protection is part of the political game. The "haves" want to protect what they have, so they become territorial. Empires within organizations take a long time to build and in the course of time become quite resistant to being altered or dismantled. This is one of the causes of the kind of segmentation that is the enemy of institution-enhancing cross-unit teamwork. Interunit teamwork, now a necessity rather than an amenity for most companies, demands that interacting units transcend their differences. This means cooperating in institution-enhancing agendas. Beating the competition must take the place of scoring victories over one another. Of course, each unit justifies its refusal to cooperate by claiming that another unit is "interfering" with its work. Therefore, when marketing wants R&D personnel to go out to meet customers in a team effort, there is grumbling about "interfering with research," "failure to understand the needs of an R&D department," "short-term thinking," and the like. While there may be some truth in these allegations, the reaction also stems from fear that the empire is about to be dismembered or become a mere satellite to another organizational unit.

The new CEO of one company took a novel approach at the first meeting of his management council. He had them sit in a predetermined order at a round table. In front of each was a title plate indicating the function he headed. After emphasizing the importance of interunit teamwork and how important it was for everyone at that table to take a general management rather than a head-of-unit view of the business, he asked each to pass the title plate in front of him to his right. In one stroke each of these executives headed a different function.

In participative management and employee involvement approaches, empowering everyone in the organization in terms of both productivity and quality of work life is the goal. People who feel empowered in some realistic way, the theory goes, tend to "get on with it" more effectively than those who wait to read the decrees, lips, or mind of the leader. Serving the leader, or rather the head, is not the same as serving the business. Of course, such empowerment is not the same as democracy. It is unrealistic to leave the final formulation of company strategy to the masses, but many people can contribute to the formulation of strategy. Having contributed, they recognize the strategy as their own and tend to implement it more vigorously than they would have without any involvement. Therefore, there is a set of principles around empowerment, though each company or institution has to come up with its own worker empowerment formulas. The empowerment process in a mental health agency will probably be quite different from that in an aircraft maintenance department of an airline.

Self-Interest Versus Institutional Enhancement

A distinction can be drawn between two kinds of politics even though in practice they are intermingled: the politics of individual or group self-interest and advancement and the politics of institutional enhancement. Unalloyed versions of the former are usually negative, while the politics of institutional advancement can be quite positive. Thus the distinction between positive and negative politics: positive politics enhance, while negative politics limit both productivity and quality of work life. If I want to put my man or woman in a position simply because he or she is "my person," even though someone else would be better for the institution, then I am into the politics of self-interest. On the other hand, if I have a candidate for a job who I believe is the best person for that job, then my fighting for him or her is an instance of the politics of institutional enhancement.

The Politics of Self-Interest. The motivation behind vying for scarce resources, on the part of either an individual or a group, can be self-interest. According to a survey reported in the *Wall Street Journal* ("The Checkoff," 1991), more than 50 percent of those polled in a national survey picked "personal ambition and motivation" as the top trait for getting ahead. Only 2 percent cited "dedication to the organization." We live in a highly individualistic society. Politics, from one perspective, then, is about the pursuit of vested interests. One of the reasons unions were founded was to protect their members against companies who pursued their interests at the expense of those of the workers. The stakes were justice and human decency. Later some of these same unions were using their power to protect the economic gains of their members, not against the onslaught of management but against relatively disadvantaged individuals or groups who were looking for their fair share of the economic pie. That is, some unions ended up doing the same kinds of things that they were formed to fight.

The politics of self-interest can play out on a national scale, in the East as well as in the West. In Japan, consumers pay much more for food in the highly protected Japanese agricultural market, and yet farmers' income is quite modest. This has something to do with huge agricultural cooperatives. Nokyo is one of them. This cooperative — assets of $447 billion, including a bank that is larger than Citicorp, a network of over thirty-five hundred local cooperatives, and a workforce of some 380,000 —

exercises a controlling influence over many of Japan's farms. Japanese farmers are beginning to grumble, although softly because of fear of reprisals, that Nokyo, as one farmer put it, "is a socialist organization that is more interested in promoting its own empire than in helping farmers" (Eisenstodt, 1991, p. 84). Nokyo provides not only fertilizer, animal feed, pesticides, and cardboard boxes (at high prices because of the tortuous distribution system) but also loans, insurance, cars, and gasoline and, like many Japanese organizations, social amenities such as marriage halls. Cooperatives exist to provide benefits for their members. Although Nokyo does this in a number of ways, it has become an empire. Empires rise because, at least initially, they serve the real needs of their constituents. Empire builders, however, often end up by putting their own interests first. That is probably why history is filled with the fall of empires.

The Politics of Institutional Enhancement. For some, political office is about opportunities for service. This is positive politics, the politics of institutional advancement. Some individuals and groups compete for scarce resources and push their own particular ideology and agendas because they believe that this is in the best interests of the institution. Take money. A company has only so much money for capital investment. An R&D group may lobby senior managers on a particular project or product, not to expand their kingdom but because they believe that the product or project will enhance the fortunes of the company and its employees. Managers in manufacturing offer a competing scenario. They believe that the expansion and globalization of the company's commodity business is the key to the future. They want money for plant expansion, new equipment, and the exploration of lucrative joint ventures with foreign companies. This is a case of competing strategic ideologies. While the winners will profit if their approach to strategy is chosen, winning and self-interest are not the central drivers. The starting point for positive politics is an institution-enhancing agenda. The end point is the value that comes from implementing that agenda.

Picture a political continuum. At one end the motivation is pure self-interest. Vested interests are to be pursued even if this means limiting or, in extreme cases, even destroying the company. The pages of business journals are filled with examples of executives who became rich at the expense of their companies. At the other end of the continuum, the motivation is the advancement of the institution. A researcher in one company made a discovery that he thought could be turned into a very profitable business. His ideas were ignored, but he pursued them out of scientific conviction. One year a plant that could be used for, among other things, making this product was up for sale at a bargain price. Another visionary convinced management that this was too good a deal to let go by. A somewhat reluctant decision was made to buy it. Subsequently, the new product was made, became a hit, and was turned into a very profitable business. Just before retirement, the researcher was recognized for his contributions and given a somewhat paltry monetary prize. The recognition, however long deferred, was greatly appreciated by the researcher. And money was not really the issue. There were many others like him in the company — people who were very loyal to it and who worked hard to advance its fortunes. They were a long way from the vested-interests end of the continuum.

On the more positive side is the experience of a vice president of a division of a larger company. He asked a consultant to review part of the division's overall strategy with him and his team. The president of the division had indicated his opposition to one key point in the strategy. The vice president and his associates were convinced that the part of the strategy that argued for a deeper push into a particular commodity market made sound business sense. The president was convinced that the future of the company lay in high-tech specialty products and tended to dismiss any kind of commodity approach. The team thought their commodity approach would complement the high-tech push, providing cash for further research and development. Since the consultant knew the president, he helped the team develop a way of selling their point of view to him. During discussions, he pointed out what seemed to an outsider to be flaws in the strategy itself. The team redid the strategy, presented it to the management committee, which was chaired by the president, and got the go-ahead. Both the president and the team had the interests of the company at heart.

Managing the Political System

As in other forms of the arational, awareness — of both one's own political inclinations and the ways in which politics are played out in the company — is the first step in managing it. Other things being equal, choosing for managerial positions people who gravitate toward the institution-enhancement end of the continuum is a second step. Often managers are chosen for their overall competence or technical skills with little attention paid to the kind of political animals they may be. A highly skilled manager who is deep into the politics of self-interest may prove dangerous indeed.

Managers committed to the development of institution-enhancing agendas and aware of the political mix within the company or institution can juggle political realities so that, in the end, they favor institutional development. Such managers do not fire those into the politics of self-interest; they monitor them. There is no reason why those who tilt to the self-interest end of the continuum cannot contribute to the common good. Effective managers do not mindlessly concentrate power in their own hands or just as mindlessly distribute it. Rather, they try to put power in the hands of those who will use it to promote institutional agendas in conjunction with quality of work life. While embracing the philosophy behind participative management and employee involvement, they still make sure that decisions serve the institution. Good managers know that disenfranchisement leads to poor, institution-limiting quality of work life. The disenfranchised have ideas and skills that are not being put to use.

Finally, effective managers know that they may have to lose some political battles for the sake of longer-term gains. The president of a division of a large corporation allowed the director of R&D, a well-connected player of the corporate game, to build a new lab that was slightly larger and more sophisticated than necessary. The president then demanded that the director develop an R&D strategy derived from and linked to the new divisional strategy. Using his team of researchers to do publishable research was the director's forte. He used the extra capacity of the lab to integrate several orphan research projects located around the country. The final package served the interests of the company.

Here is a process one senior management team used to "do politics," that is, to set up a political campaign, in an institution-enhancing way.

- *Institution-enhancing agendas.* Everyone who wanted something that consumed scarce resources — people, money, time, and so forth — had to demonstrate how the new project would benefit the business. This was the nonnegotiable starting point.
- *Political philosophy.* The team outlined acceptable values in doing politics — how to play, as it were. No lies, no inflated budgets, no asking for A because you wanted to do B, no sabotaging your opponents, no working underground. Politics were to be pursued with human decency.
- *Stakeholder audit.* All those who would be affected by the proposal or project were identified. This included, for instance, managers who had to sign off on the project and individuals or groups essential to implementing the project.
- *Targeted stakeholders.* Key stakeholders, especially those who could influence other stakeholders, were identified, together with their interests.
- *Strategy audit.* Strategies for influencing key stakeholders were reviewed. These included appeals to reason, trade-offs, coalition formation, emotional appeals — the whole gamut of things politicians do to get people to join a cause.
- *The plan.* A package of strategies that had the highest probability for success were put together in a plan. Strategies that failed the values test were eliminated.
- *The campaign.* The plan was executed. Key stakeholders were contacted and lobbied. Meetings were held to discuss what was working and what was not. Tactical changes in the plan were discussed and implemented.

There are simpler and more elaborate versions of this process. It is possible to do all of it in half an hour. Obviously it should not consume more time and energy than the value it adds. But if the starting point is an agenda that the proponents believe will add substantive value to the enterprise, then doing the politics necessary to make it happen is simply part of the job.

Culture: "The Way We Do Things Here"

The culture of a company or institution is the fifth shadow side area. In some ways it is more important than all the other shadow side dimensions combined. Institutional culture ("the way we do things here") has been called the largest and most controlling of the systems. It permeates all the activities of companies and institutions, giving them individuality and color. It is called the "most controlling of the systems" because it dictates the norms for doing everything—all business, organizational, managerial, and leadership master tasks and subtasks.

Culture also dictates the norms for the other shadow side categories. It dictates how messy or "loosely coupled" things may be. In many educational systems, the prevalent culture allows staff members to put self-serving organizational agendas ahead of student-serving business agendas. The culture also dictates norms for individual behavior. For instance, it tells us how crazy we can be and still remain members of our respective organizations. The culture of IBM is probably less tolerant of individual idiosyncrasies than the culture of, say, some start-up computer firm making IBM clones. A person moving from a start-up firm to IBM would probably experience a degree of "culture shock." Culture lays down norms for the social system. In some institutions you have to be an engineer to rise to the top. There is no ironclad rule, of course, it is just the way things are. Culture tells us what kind of politics are allowed and just how members of an organization are allowed to play the political game. In one large British company, self-interest agendas were the name of the game. "If this does not help me and my career, why should I do it?" For years managers routinely manipulated budgets to pursue personal and career goals. All this changed when a recession hit and this company's particular industry went into convulsions.

As a major source of both system-enhancing and system-limiting arationality, organizational culture has received a great deal of theoretical and practical attention over the last decade. However, culture, like many other things in life, is easier to talk about than to manage.

Case Study: Understanding and Managing Culture

Some years ago I was working with one of the Bell companies. After the divestiture from AT&T, there was some need to determine what kind of culture was needed in the new, much more competitive world into which the Baby Bells were moving. I had been contacted by the vice president of the human resource department because he had heard that I was doing some work in organizational culture. He said that fashioning a culture that served the business was one of the primary tasks of the company. In fact, it was so important that the company's president had indicated that he himself would take the leadership role in transforming the culture. The vice president indicated that the senior managers of the company discussed the culture regularly at their executive committee meetings.

I said that I had two hypotheses. The first was that each of these gentlemen — and the culture at the time pretty much dictated that they be gentlemen — had his own idea of what culture was since together they probably had not had the time to determine some common working definition and model of culture. A slight smile crossed his face. "My second hypothesis," I said, "is that all of these personal understandings of culture are somewhat vague." The smile broadened. I asked why I was talking to him rather than to the president, since the latter had assigned culture to himself. He hemmed and hawed a bit and then said that "a lot of it" had been delegated to him because the president was "so busy." I learned something about the culture. If culture is something vague, then it is difficult to manage, and CEOs and other senior managers will not find the time to take a lead role in managing it. Therefore, it is very useful for managers to have a working definition and model of culture, even if it is as simple as "the way we do things here."

Shared Beliefs, Values, and Norms That Drive Behavior

Culture can be understood and ultimately managed through the following three categories:

1. shared *patterns of behavior* — "our way of doing things,"
2. shared *beliefs, values, norms* — "our way of thinking,"
3. organizational *underpinnings* — "what we reward and punish around here."

     The categories are overlapping and interactive; beliefs, values, and norms are what drive the shared patterns of behavior, which are kept in place by the organizational underpinnings. And, while each of these has its importance, the best starting point is the institution's "way of doing things."
     The bottom line of culture is the habitual ways of carrying out business, organizational, managerial, supervisory, and leadership tasks and activities. A manager might say, "Though there are no ironclad rules about it, we have always promoted people on the basis of merit rather than seniority." Another might say, "Strategy is king around here. If you make money in your business unit but do so by violating the strategy, you will be called for it. If you're unclear about how to translate the strategy into your set of operations, you had better clear it up quickly." These managers are talking about patterns of behavior. Culture deals with patterns, not isolated behaviors.

Model A and "The Way We Do Things Here"

Culture permeates every dimension of a company or institution. Every institution has a business culture ("the way we do strategy around here" or "the way we pursue quality around here"); there is an organizational culture ("the way we make decisions around here" or "the way we recruit people around here"); there is a managerial culture ("the way managers spend their time around here"); there is a supervisory culture ("the way supervisors relate to employees around here"); there is a leadership culture ("the way we get business-enhancing change going around here"). In other words, culture permeates every kind of activity in the company or institution.

Culture as Institution Limiting. Here are some examples of institution-limiting "ways we do things here," taken from the six categories of Model A:

- *Strategy.* "We formulate strategy here, but then do little about it. It has always just floated on the top."
- *Operations.* "We give lip service to customer service but never really do anything about it. We're no better than anyone else."
- *Structure.* "We continually let the decision-making process drag on and on here. At times it seems that no one is in charge."
- *Human resource management systems.* "We don't take recruitment very seriously here. We think that we can make anyone fit in. And we don't seem to learn from our mistakes."
- *Management and supervision.* "You don't need people-related skills around here. If in doubt, be tough. No manager has even been fired for not listening to good ideas from his subordinates."
- *Leadership.* "When leadership below the executive level emerges here, we quash it. Don't get too far out in front of the boss. In fact, stay close behind."

Culture as Institution Enhancing. Culture can also be institution enhancing in a wide variety of ways. Here are some examples on the positive side:

- *Strategy.* "We tend to formulate strategy here by tapping into the wisdom of those middle managers who will be responsible for implementing it. Their ideas are just as important as those of the ultimate decision makers."
- *Operations.* "It's taken a long time, but just about everyone

around here thinks quality now. It's in the bones and marrow of the company."

- *Structure.* "We don't pay much attention to the organizational boxes here. We get things done even if we have to move across organizational lines."
- *Human resource management systems.* "Development around here is a process rather than a program. Just about every manager rises to what has been called the development challenge. The value of our human assets increases every year."
- *Management and supervision.* "While most of our managers are smart, quite a few are also wise. They monitor shadow side realities around here and try to get them to serve the institution."
- *Leadership.* "Everyone around here tries to improve the work on his or her unit. Constant improvement has become a way of thinking and doing for us."

Beliefs, Values, and Norms That Drive Ways of Acting

Beliefs, values, and norms — "the way we think around here" — constitute the cognitive part of culture, while shared patterns of behavior — "the way we do things around here" — constitute the behavioral or action part. Beliefs and assumptions interact with values and become institutionalized in the culture as norms, the characteristic patterns of behavior found in the organization. Here is what happened in one company.

- *Belief.* There was a belief, probably based on some experience, that bosses did not want to hear bad news and tended to punish bearers of bad news.
- *Value.* One of the primary values operating in the organization was security.
- *Norm.* The norm was, "If anything goes wrong, look the other way. If you can't look the other way, don't tell anyone about it."

Of course, this norm stifled communication and had an unnoticed negative impact on productivity. Nothing was done about this until a TQM program was introduced. The consultants soon discovered the buried norm and challenged it publicly. They pointed out that people needed to be rewarded for ferreting out processes and procedures that stood in the way of doing things right the first time.

In another company, the belief-value-norm pattern looked like this:

- *Belief.* "In the eyes of our bosses, we are only as good as the results we produce today. Yesterday's results are forgotten. Tomorrow's are not here yet."
- *Value.* "Get ahead. The place is filled with professionals who want to be on the fast track."
- *Norms.* "Be flashy. Produce short-term results. Fudge the figures a bit. Find out what's on your boss's immediate agenda and help him do that."

This, too, was a deadly combination, introducing a short-term mentality and militating against the longer-term pursuit of strategy. There was a cutthroat atmosphere in the place.

Some organizations are very conservative. Since they prize stability, risk-taking behaviors do not abound. A standard norm might be, "Be careful what you do with the assets of this company. If you err, err on the safe side." The trouble with such an injunction, of course, is that the company's competitors may well be taking risks and winning. In this case, the conservative norms of the institution are doing it in.

Underpinnings: Keeping the Culture in Place

Once the culture takes root in the system, it tends to stay there, even when it does not serve the system well. That is, the beliefs, values, and norms that drive behavior tend to be stable over time. Since the cognitive dimensions of culture—beliefs, values, and norms—are often covert, they are not easily accessible to change. Several interactive factors keep culture in place whether it serves the institution or not: adaptation, lack of cultural awareness, inertia, the incentive and reward system, the self-interest of those who benefit from the status quo, and control processes and procedures of various kinds. For instance, it does little to preach a culture of risk taking in an organization where it is not rewarded and mistakes, including those made in taking risks, are routinely punished. If a company has difficulty creating a new culture that will serve the business better, two questions to be asked are, What's keeping the old culture in place? What are the rewards for the behaviors called for by the new culture?

One large professional institution was trying to cut down on the amount of paper it produced. Edicts came forth from the president's office to this effect, but year after year the mountain of paper seemed to grow even larger. One problem was that it was difficult to find a document that did not have the word *draft* on it. Draft version succeeded draft version. There were two major underpinnings: professionalism carried to an extreme and pride mixed with fear. There were many world-class professionals in this organization, and they set very high standards. Therefore, everything had to be done perfectly even though this kind of extreme perfectionism did not serve the business. Second, though they would not admit it, these professionals feared criticism from one another. The term *draft* warded off that criticism, at least to an extent. People could say, "Well, these were a few ideas I quickly threw together." As long as the president focused on just the mounds of paper, nothing would change. The paper was a symptom, not the problem.

Dimensions of Culture

Organizational culture has a number of dimensions that help managers both understand and manage it, that is, help make it serve both the business and quality of work life more effectively.

Overt and Covert Cultures. Overt culture refers to the beliefs, values, and norms that are publicly espoused by an institution. For instance, many companies say, "Our people constitute our most important asset." On the other hand, covert or hidden beliefs, values, and norms constitute the shadow side of the culture.

In one company there was a covert norm that said, "Don't promote a woman to a position unless you are absolutely sure that she will be significantly better than any man being considered for that position." This norm obviously was not discussed in the public forums of the institution. Covert beliefs, values, and norms, even though they exercise a great deal of influence on everything that goes on within an organization, can be quite difficult to uncover, often because there is a further covert norm that says, "This topic is not to be discussed. Discuss the undiscussables of this company at your own peril."

In one company, a consultant asked a group of middle managers to list on a sheet of paper hidden or undiscussed norms that they thought interfered with the business. The list they produced was substantial. It included such norms as, "If anything goes wrong, find someone else to blame as quickly as possible" and "Never let your boss know that there is something you are supposed to know but do not know." When these were put up on flip charts, the consultant asked, "Is there anything you can do about these?" They all cried, "Of course we can!" One added, "If we work together." The point is that not all covert dysfunctional beliefs, values, and norms are so deeply buried that an archeologist is needed to uncover them. Once uncovered, these dysfunctional norms can be challenged and changed. This is not to say that changing a company's culture is a piece of cake. It does challenge the assumption that culture always takes years to change, if it can be changed at all.

Espoused Culture Versus Actual Culture. Just because an organization states its beliefs in some public way does not mean that it acts on them. What people actually do in an organization tells us what the organization really believes, prizes, and encourages. One company included technology among its major values— "we are a company driven by creativity in technology"—but consistently allowed its competitors to develop and maintain a technological edge. Nor do high-sounding statements about people lead automatically to effective quality of work life practices. One company that proclaimed it was in the "people" business was infamous for the way it set aside quality of work life considerations at the first signs of an economic downturn.

A social service center claimed that its staff members constituted its most important resource, but managers provided
them with little positive feedback, resisted innovative ideas that
came from staff, and had an unarticulated expectation that staff
members would put in more hours than they were paid for. The
espoused value — championing human assets — was not a value-
in-use; it had little impact on managerial behavior. In these cases
it is clear that there was a set of covert values and norms that
took precedence over publicly stated values and norms.

In one company the new president said to the troops,
"There are a number of cultural paradigms that do not serve
us well. It is time that we name them so that we can do something about them. We say one thing and we do another. This
is sapping the vitality of this company. When it comes to values
and norms, we can no longer afford to keep two sets of books."
Two years later they were still struggling with dysfunctional
paradigms, but there had been much progress. For instance,
there were two women on the company's internal board of directors. This does not mean that they had solved the "women are
less" problem, but they were struggling with it more honestly.
One of the president's most influential statements was, "It's not
my job to change our culture. We are all carriers of that culture. And so it is everyone's job."

Strong and Weak Cultures. Cultures are strong if the company's
beliefs, values, and norms consistently drive behavior. For instance, if the espoused norm is, "Make strategy the guide in
everything you do," but many managers still maintain an operational rather than a strategic mind-set — just getting the day-
to-day work done — then, with respect to implementing strategy,
the espoused or preferred culture is weak. In one company, the
espoused norm is, "We are a strategy-driven company." In this
company managers seldom speak about the business without
referring to the strategy. Strategy consistently drives behavior.
The culture, with respect to getting the strategy to drive the business, is strong.

Unfortunately, dysfunctional covert norms can also consistently drive behavior. In one institution there was a covert
belief and norm package that stated, "We are hired as individuals

and we work as individuals. We are also rewarded as individuals. Therefore, rule number one is, Watch out for yourself. No one else will. Keep out of other people's way. When a TQM process that called for extensive teamwork was tried in the company, it failed miserably. The strong covert culture persisted.

Managing Culture

Managing the organizational culture does not usually appear as an item on the job specification for the average manager, but it probably should, because fashioning and maintaining a culture that serves the business adds value. The overall culture management task may be stated as follows:

Make every effort to ensure that the culture both serves the business, including strategy and operations, and enhances the quality of work life.

When Delta Air Lines moved into the international arena, some industry analysts doubted that the company would compete effectively with airlines such as United and American because of its culture of caution. The international arena demanded boldness, and both United and American were daring. Therefore, it was up to Delta's managers to make sure that the culture would support its new strategy. As of this writing, Delta has not been very successful in international travel, but it is hard to judge why. The company entered the market at the wrong time, and a lingering recession has been doing in all U.S. carriers. However, it may also be that culture needs to be more effectively aligned with the business.

Managing culture involves three principal tasks: auditing the culture, promoting the preferred culture, and challenging and changing dimensions of the culture that do not serve productivity and quality of work life.

The Culture Audit. Managers need to be "ethnographers," that is, they need to know the beliefs, values, and norms, especially the covert norms, under which the natives, themselves included, operate. While in recent years there has been a push toward formal culture audits, there is some concern about how these audits are structured. Formal culture audits target culture in and of itself, whereas culture, as noted above, is embedded in all the behaviors of the institution. Culture is not just another box on the organizational chart. Informal culture audits that focus on the beliefs, values, and norms behind or embedded in patterns of business, organizational, and managerial behavior would seem to make more sense. In other words, a manager's "taking the pulse of the system" through Model A should include a reading of the embedded culture and the degree to which the culture is currently serving the business.

There are many different ways of getting at the covert culture. For instance, persistent or intractable problems such as the "too much paper around here" problem outlined earlier are windows onto the culture. That is, persistent problems are often culture problems. In one company customer service programs continually failed. No matter how hard managers preached, little progress was made. Finally, at a meeting one manager said, "We see customer service as soft. And we are not good at soft things. We're good at engineering and marketing. These are substantial, these are tough. Until we change our attitude toward so-called soft things, we're not going to make much progress. We're not going to pursue what we don't respect."

Promoting the Preferred Culture. In a start-up, whether it is a new business or a new unit or some new project within an existing business, managers benefit from being able to fashion a culture that serves the business right from the beginning. The strategic building blocks of mission, vision, and values provide a useful starting point. The 1988 Olympics were an outstanding success in part because the organizers, under the leadership of Peter Ueberroth, fashioned a culture to support the mammoth venture and got workers and volunteers to buy into it. General Motors started Saturn as a separate business precisely to fashion a culture different from the staid and inflexible one emanating from Detroit. While there was some doubt about whether it would be possible to fashion a different culture, in 1992 Saturn was doing very well. Critics were wondering why some of the culture changes were not being exported to the rest of General Motors. The more cynical said, "Detroit casts a very long shadow. Let's wait and see what happens to Saturn."

Managers of established concerns with a culture already in place must find a range of ways of promoting the preferred culture. This, of course, assumes that there is a preferred culture. If there is none, one must be formulated. Once formulated, it must be continually reinforced. At Montgomery Ward there is a strong culture, and the CEO, Bernard Brennan, takes every meeting as an opportunity to reinforce both the company's strategy and its business culture. "We do the right things the low-cost way" is a message that is pounded in over and over again. "Whatever it takes to improve the business" is another. Managers in all companies and institutions can add value by asking themselves again and again, "What do I need to do to reinforce the dimensions of the culture that best serve the business?" One answer lies in making sure that the underpinnings such as the incentive and reward system support the preferred culture both in policy and in practice.

Cultural maintenance includes continually "tweaking the culture" when it gets out of line. After a successful year in one small company, the president noted that travel expenses were creeping up. Even though the espoused culture was one of cost containment, success had spawned a covert norm, "It's all right to start living high on the hog if you're successful." The company was in a highly competitive industry. Cost containment provided a competitive edge. In a management meeting, the president had the managers restate some of the central norms of the preferred culture. He then reviewed the quarter's travel expenses. Travel expenses went down substantially in the next quarter.

Challenging and Changing the Culture. In the early 1990s, facing a substantial downturn in profits in the face of stiff competition, IBM began examining and trying to change its own culture. Somehow, the "way we do things here" was no longer serving the business. IBM needed a new way of doing things. It had to become more flexible and more nimble to retain its stature. A 90 percent plunge in profits in the second quarter of 1991 underscored the problem. The CEO of IBM, in an internal memo, took people to task for their complacency. A culture of complacency was the last thing a computer company needed in moving through the 1990s into the even more turbulent twenty-first century.

Changing a deeply rooted culture that has not served the business for years is a much more formidable challenge. Managers of such companies as AT&T, once the safe harbor of regulation was left behind, had to do a culture audit to identify the business-limiting beliefs, values, and norms of the entrenched culture, challenge them, formulate a preferred culture, and find ways of getting the preferred culture entrenched in the system. This was to be a longer-term process because deep-seated assumptions, beliefs, values, and norms were at stake, and they would not readily be changed. An entire institutional mind-set had to be transformed.

When Bob Allen became the new CEO of AT&T, he knew that challenging and changing the culture would be one of the most difficult but one of the most important of his tasks. The various units of the telecommunications giant needed to become more customer-focused and to develop internal supplier-to-customer relationships. This required the units to develop a new mode of discourse with one another ("the way we talk with one another around here"). The employees had to begin to discuss the undiscussables. For instance, internal customers began telling internal suppliers precisely what was wrong with their wares and service. This in itself was a remarkable culture change. Early successes were important, but Allen knew, however, that it would take a long time to transform the culture. But the culture had to change to support the company's new global strategy. The trick was getting the workforce to support culture change efforts.

Like death and taxes or the sex-lies-politics package, shadow side realities will always be with us. The shadow side adds challenging richness, complexity, and depth to both individual and institutional life; struggles with the shadow side often bring out the best in both. While the shadow side adds complexity to Models A and B, understanding the shadow side helps managers use these models more intelligently and effectively. Though suggestions about identifying and managing shadow side realities have been made, the principal question still persists — can we manage the shadow side of the system as outlined here? The naïve person may say, "Certainly, it's just a question of giving managers the right tools." The pure cynic will respond, "No way! We can only watch the show." The realist will probably say, "Yes we can, at least to a point. . . . How much of it can we manage? Certainly enough to make a difference."

SEVEN

Initiating and
Managing Change

The principal theme of this book is that managers add value by responding to the needs of the business. They need certain skills to do so, but these skills are not ends in themselves. Change is often one of the needs of the business. Armed with a viable method for change and the ability and wisdom to use it well, managers are in a position to add value.

An Advanced Organizer: What Chapter Seven Is About

- *From Stagnation to Creativity.* Businesses need change both to survive and thrive. Model B, which is about initiation and managing change, deals with critical needs of the business.
- *The Model B Framework.* Model B is at once a problem-solving model, a crisis-management model, a model for managing environmental change, a model for initiating internal change, and a model for managing the fallout from change.
- *The Shadow Side of Model B.* Discretionary change has a poor track record in human affairs. The shadow side of change — the messy, emotional, socially disruptive, political, and countercultural aspects — contributes greatly to this poor track record.
- *The Stages of Model B.* The Model B process includes analyzing

133

the current scenario, developing a preferred scenario, selecting strategies for moving from the current to the preferred,
and developing a "bias for action."

- *The Shadow Side Revisited.* Action has impediments. Three
  major ones are overload, inertia, and entropy.

From Stagnation to Creativity

Too many companies, institutions, and agencies fail to create
the kind of climate of vigilance and innovation that would enable them to renew themselves in the face of "environmental"
turbulence. We all know companies and institutions that have
"congealed into their final selves." They still go on, but they offer
little interest to those who come in contact with them and little
challenge to whose who work in them. Their continued survival
in the face of turbulent environments is open to question.

Different Kinds of Change

The problem with the cliché "The only constant these days is
change" is that it is becoming more and more true. There are
three important aspects of managing change. First, managers
need to deal with the impact of change that is taking place in
the company's environment and affecting the business. They
have to become much more responsive to customers, more flexible in organizational structures, and much quicker to bring
products to market because the competition is breathing down
their neck. Second, managers need to actively initiate changes
to constantly improve the business. For instance, retailers must
move into creating new forms of retailing in a day when "me
too" approaches go nowhere. Third, managers must cope with
the fallout from the changes they institute. The upstart low-price
mail-order computer companies such as Dell and Gateway have
caused the "big guys" like IBM and DEC and Compaq to play
the clone, mail-order, and low-price games themselves. Now
the upstarts have to factor these reactions into their strategies.

Managing the Impact of Environmental Change. The economy
goes into a slump, competitors come out with better products,

new technologies give others a competitive edge in manufacturing, or the workforce grows older and more diverse. Managers need a process that enables them to manage the impact of change on the institution. If specialty retailing is sweeping the country, what is an old-line department store to do? This kind of management of change is reactive. Something happens that affects us or will affect us down the line and we need to cope with the challenge. The airline and automobile industries have been beset by this kind of change for years. Those that fail to meet the challenge to change fall by the wayside. The intensity of external change differs from industry to industry and waxes and wanes in many different ways. But no company or institution is immune, not even the not-for-profits such as government, education, and church.

Initiating Change. There are various reasons for making changes, even when not absolutely forced to do so: the desire to be an industry leader, the desire to continually improve performance and increase profitability, the desire to improve the quality of work life, even the fascination with innovation itself. In the computer industry, instituting change in order to stay on the cutting edge in terms of either technological or marketing prowess is commonplace. Toshiba took the lead in notebook computer technology only to discover that its rivals were hard at work designing notebooks with even more advanced technology. On the other hand, educational systems, blessed with hundreds of creative possibilities for change, cannot seem to get out of the starting gate. When for-profit secondary schools announce that they can offer better quality education at a lower price, many of these educational systems can do nothing more than cry foul and invoke the flag: "These new schools are robbing Americans of their precious patrimony. Competition is un-American!" Actively pursuing change is often risky, but in some industries it is absolutely essential for survival.

Managing the Fallout from Change. When companies and institutions do institute changes — develop a new strategy, move into a new line of business, downsize and streamline the workforce, introduce a new information management system — these changes often set into motion a whole set of reactions that managers need to deal with. Workers in a company that is downsizing threaten to strike, a new strategy galvanizes a sleepy competitor into action, new information upsets the tenuous political balance that existed between departments. Sometimes the fallout from change can be predicted, sometimes not. Therefore, companies need a culture of vigilance and the ability to respond quickly to crises.

Model B deals with the need of companies and institutions for various kinds of change. Managers need frameworks, tools, and skills to become adept at managing all these kinds of change. Model B provides both a framework for directing change and methods to make the management of change serve the interests of both the institution and its stakeholders.

Leadership and Change

To suggest that "change is the only constant" is a recent phenomenon would be erroneous. Over one hundred years ago John Cardinal Newman expressed the same sentiment in a more literary way: "In a higher world it is otherwise, but here below to live is to change, and to be perfect is to have changed often." Leading-edge organizations do not change for the sake of change. Rather they change by discovering and adopting options that add value to the business and by dropping practices that do not. This is the heart of learning—the discovery and implementation of value-added options. In times of economic, social, and political turbulence — and which era of human history has been without these? — the ability of a system to renew itself is critical. Leadership, as outlined in Chapter Five, is about improving the business. This involves initiating and managing innovation and change.

If the managers and workers in a learning organization are expected to participate in the leadership process, they — each in his or her own way — need to become, as Kanter (1983) suggested, "change masters" or "corporate entrepreneurs." In any given company such sentiments may, of course, constitute no more than glassy-eyed idealism, forgotten by most in the give-

and-take of everyday business. Companies and institutions that find ways of translating these ideals into everyday reality will face current and future turbulence better than most.

Three things are needed for change leadership. First, the institution must be sincerely interested in institution-enhancing change. Second, managers must be empowered to initiate change and in turn empower others. Third, the "tools" of change must be available. One essential tool is routinely neglected — a simple but comprehensive model of initiating and managing innovation and change that is shared throughout the institution. Model B, which presents such a framework, is the third and final model of the "shared models of managing" package. It can be used by anyone to take an active part in the leadership process that characterizes learning organizations.

The Model B Framework

Model B, a model for initiating and managing change, is an extremely important managerial tool because of its versatility. It is at once a problem-solving model, an opportunity-development model, a crisis management model, a model for managing the impact of environmental changes that are beyond the control of the institution, a model for initiating business, organizational, and managerial change, a model for managing the fallout from instituted change, and even a coaching and counseling model. Even though there are books on each of these processes, it helps to know that all tend to be variations of a core process. Model B presents this core process in three stages:

1. *The current scenario* assesses the current state of affairs.
2. The *preferred scenario* creates a picture or map of the desired package of outcomes.
3. *Action strategies* are designed to move the system from the current to the preferred scenario.

These three steps are reinforced by a bias for action: building results-oriented action into the change process from the very beginning. Model B is illustrated in Figure 7.1. The figure makes

Figure 7.1. Model B: A Model for Organizational Change.

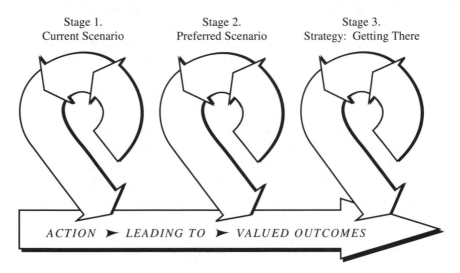

it clear that the planning that occurs in stages one through three should drive action right from the beginning.

Since most change projects seem to lose momentum or "action" along the way, there is a need to stress meaningful action and build it into the change process from the start. This is not a call for action for the sake of action. Meaningful action has two characteristics: it has direction, that is, it is oriented toward the value-added goals and objectives of the preferred end state, and it is prudent.

The Major Stages of Model B

The major stages of Model B seek to address a series of important questions.

1.   Current Scenario. What's going on? What are our current problems and challenges? What opportunities need developing?

For instance, the senior managers of one computer company put it this way, "What is our principal challenge? It's this: our main competitor has just come out with a simpler, faster, and less expensive desktop computer. It is better than the one we currently have on the drawing board."

The needed change in this instance is planning and implementing a timely and substantive response to the initiatives of a competitor.

2.   Preferred Scenario. *What should be in place rather than what's currently in place? What would things look like if they looked better?*

The company's planning team asked themselves, "What would our best response to the competition look like?" After looking at their options, they responded, "Bringing out a look-alike desktop computer will not do the trick. However, coming out with a fast and reasonably priced notebook computer that can also serve as a desktop will put us back into contention. We already have a notebook in the design process. Within five months we will bring out a redesigned version of our notebook computer that is just as fast as their desktop."

3.   Action Strategies. *What do we have to do to move from the current to the preferred scenario? What would the best package of strategies be? What are the critical steps? What would a plan that is both feasible but flexible look like?*

The planning team came to the following conclusions: "The design for the current notebook isn't quite finished. So we will get the design team together with the people from manufacturing, marketing, and sales to mount a product development and marketing blitz. Since our figures show us that projected sales and profits warrant overtime, we will run flat out. Five months is an incredibly short time, but we have the resources and the will to meet the deadline."

To build results-oriented action into the process of every step, the team asked, "What can we do immediately to start moving toward the preferred scenario? How do we make sure that planning right from the start leads to outcome-focused and productive action?"

The company's integrated "blitz" team mandated some immediate steps: "We will immediately notify key suppliers to advance the delivery dates of the notebook components. If they can't deliver, we'll seek out alternate suppliers. We will cancel the advertising programs we had in place for our desktops and put our advertisers on notice that we will need a new campaign. We will immediately put on sale some of our best-selling desktop models."

Note two things in this simplified example. First, this is an example of initiating change in response to some change in the environment. It is reactive. The company was caught off guard. If there had been a better process in place for keeping track of the competition or if the company itself had been more aggressive in terms of new-product development, then this whole scene might have been avoided. Second, as it works its way through the technology of change, the company must also ask, What will the fallout of this change project be and how will we manage it? For instance, many people will be asked on short notice to put in considerable overtime. The members of the blitz team, therefore, might say something like this: "We need to set up a general meeting of our workers and explain both the threat and the opportunity in such a way as to get enthusiastic buy-in from them."

The Shadow Side of Model B

Change has a shadow side. Companies and institutions that commit themselves to being on the cutting edge in their respective lines of business understand the following fact and weave its wisdom into all their change projects: discretionary change has a very poor track record in human affairs. The simple fact is, if people or institutions do not have to change, they do not change. This is not pessimism or cynicism; it is reality. Witness our New Year's resolutions. They seldom amount to much. The more cynical would say that they do not have a chance. Statistics from both the United States and Australia show that over 75 percent of quality management programs fail.

The shadow side of change encompasses the five generic categories of Model C outlined in Chapter Six: organizational messiness, individuals and their idiosyncrasies, the company's social system, the politics of the institution, and the institution's culture. The general principle is quite simple:

Change, whether individual or institutional, is messy, emotional, social, political, and cultural or countercultural in nature. These realities need to be factored into the change process from the very beginning.

The shadow side of change can, with uncanny ease, sabotage even the best-planned and best-intentioned change effort. To ignore the shadow side is to court failure.

The five shadow side factors are explored through a case adapted from a real company in a real situation. This consulting company specialized in designing and installing state-of-the-art computer-based information systems. These new systems often had a profound impact on both the business and the organizational realities of the firm's clients. While the company was renowned for its technical expertise, it was often faulted for ignoring the human side of technological change. To remedy this, the partners set up a division that specialized in the human side of change. The members of this unit worked with both their own information technology professionals and with clients in order to make the introduction of the new information systems go as smoothly as possible. However, while the professionals in this division had a range of "people" skills and an understanding of the human dimensions of the workplace, they did not have an overall framework for managing the shadow side of their interventions. Model C was proposed for this purpose.

Work with one of their clients went like this. The consulting company had landed a contract with a large service company to install a new information management system. The service company was basically in the cleanup business. Although it had started with services such as the daily cleaning of factories, stores, and office buildings and garbage removal, it had more recently added other, more sophisticated cleanup businesses, such as final cleanup of decommissioned factories, cleanup of toxic waste sites, and consulting services on waste management. It was a successful, rapidly growing company. The professional consultants who specialized in the human side of change had the burden of convincing both their own technicians and management that the added costs of managing shadow side realities up front made both short-term and long-term business sense, that it was a value-added process that would pay for itself. The management-of-change specialists at the consulting company promised their clients a smoother transition process in the short term and a more effective use of the information technology down the line.

Here is how each of the five shadow side categories related to this case.

Organizational Messiness

Change agents need to assess the degree of organizational mess-iness and its relevance to the kind of change contemplated. For instance, if a company is rapidly losing market share to com-petitors and operating in panic mode, it certainly is not the best time to mount a new management development program. Or if an institution is loosely coupled in too many ways (for instance, if a bloated and self-serving staff organization is too loosely cou-pled with the business of education in a large-city school sys-tem), then installing a new performance management system will probably go nowhere. The system is not ready for this kind of change. An audit of shadow side realities helps determine a company's readiness for change. Furthermore, change, even when absolutely necessary, often increases organizational mess-iness in the short term. This can be dangerous. Because of the increased messiness, people begin to say, "This is not working. Things around here are worse than they used to be. Let's get back to doing it the old way." History shows that some restruc-turing efforts have merely driven the final nail into a company's coffin.

The consulting company realized that the cleaning ser-vices company was growing rapidly and experiencing some of the chaos that goes along with rapid growth. While a new in-formation system was needed, the installation of the system would certainly add to the chaos in the short term. Therefore, the consultants helped the client's managers take a "forewarned is forearmed" approach. In introducing the new system, they highlighted ways in which messiness would increase and sug-gested strategies for handling it. Members of the client's own internal task force on change sat down with key managers, pointed out the kinds of messiness that would ensue, and got them to brainstorm strategies for handling it. The consulting company also developed an internal public relations and marketing program for the new information system to highlight its long-term benefits. The client's managers used this program to get buy-in from the troops.

Individuals' Idiosyncracies

Since people react quite idiosyncratically to change — some wholeheartedly embracing it, others wholeheartedly engaging in efforts to sabotage it — it is often essential to ponder how certain individuals will react to some contemplated change before the change takes place or even before it is designed. Managers seldom think of how different individuals might react to change and therefore do not formulate strategies for helping them to cope with it. It is much more likely that middle managers will blame "higher ups" for the agony associated with major change and then ask workers in their units to get on with it. They ignore the fact that key individuals can play an important role in getting the entire unit to understand, accept, "own," and implement the change.

One consultant spotted a key divisional manager, George, who she thought might try to sabotage the new system, or at least drag his feet and hinder implementation. When she shared her suspicions with Tom, his manager, he readily saw that this might be the case. Realizing that George had never been asked his opinion about the new system, Tom asked him to join the implementation task force. Tom's action was neither naïve or cynical. George was one of those people who see the world from a different angle from most and Tom sincerely thought that he would add value to the team. Tom made efforts to turn a potential adversary into an ally; or at least into a nonsaboteur. Another relatively new manager spotted two members of his unit who wholeheartedly welcomed the change. He briefed them on what was to come and then had them brief the rest of the unit. Unit members liked being briefed by people they knew.

The Social System

Change can upset the social fabric of an organization. Since people are often moved around when change is implemented, cliques and alliances are rearranged or broken up. While dysfunctional cliques may be broken up through change programs (some change programs are designed to do precisely that), it may happen that productivity-enhancing groups may have to go, and thus patterns of informal leadership may also be disrupted. Wise managers know the ways in which the social system serves the business and the ways in which it limits it. If they see that necessary change is going to cause some kind of social upheaval, they prepare for it.

While the new information system would tie all of the cleaning services company's businesses together, it would involve the decentralization of the information management department so that its members could serve the various businesses more effectively and efficiently. While the information management "clique" had been faulted for a lack of customer focus and failure to provide user-friendly systems, there had always been a great "techie" spirit among its members. They communicated very well with one another and went out of their way to help one another. Breaking up this social system could eliminate these benefits and cause trouble. To help counter the disappointments decentralization would bring, the consultants suggested that the members of the information management department be allowed a great deal of say as to who would go where. Since, in some sense, they were making their own assignments, social ties were seen to be stretched, not broken. They would form a network across the corporation. In truth, this social arrangement would serve the business much more effectively than the one it was replacing. The consulting company also provided for the line managers of the various business units workshops on what needed to be done to socialize these players into the new teams.

Organizational Politics

Politics, as has been stated, means vying for such things as power, certain ideological points of view, responsibility and authority, and scarce resources. Since change inevitably involves these factors, it is always political. The balance of power shifts, new ideologies are proposed or mandated, and scarce resources are reallocated. Many workers see substantial change as a process that creates winners and losers. And so every substantive change effort should be preceded by a stakeholder analysis, which involves

- Listing the range of stakeholders affected by the proposed changes
- Identifying key stakeholders from the list together with their principal stakes or interests
- Determining whether each stakeholder is an ally, a fence sitter, or an adversary with respect to intended changes (see Block, 1987)
- Developing strategies, preferably of the win-win variety, to deal with key stakeholders and their interests
- Factoring in stakeholder concerns right from the start

The royal route to stakeholder management is to include stakeholders in different ways in every stage of the planning and implementation process. In one company that was about to adopt a radically new strategy, a series of debates about the building blocks of a new strategy were held over a period of six months. By the time the strategy itself was promulgated, everyone recognized it because each had put his or her "smell" on it through the debates.

The cleaning services company's human resources department, led by a talented but highly ambitious vice president, saw in the decentralization of the information management department an opportunity to exert more control over the direction of the company. He had been readying a stream of human resources (HR) initiatives that would bring the company "into the twenty-first century." The company's CEO realized fully that the company had to adapt to new workforce realities, but he also knew that each HR initiative had to be linked to the business, not to the growth of an HR empire. He worked closely with the consulting firm's senior project director on strategies to prevent a wave of power struggles and to cut empire-building

efforts short. The CEO established a strategic planning committee and included the HR vice president. Part of the committee's mandate, expressed in very clear terms, was to make
sure that every initiative from every department served the
strategy. Guidelines for making sure that this linkage took place
were formulated.

Organizational Culture

Change efforts can be either supported or opposed by the prevalent culture. A culture audit may be required to determine the
norms and practices in use that will support proposed changes
and those that will stand in the way. If the proposed changes
are too countercultural, it might be better to phase them in,
mounting, in the meantime, culture change efforts.

In the old culture, sales personnel at the cleaning services
company waited for phone calls from customers requesting services. While they responded well to customer requests, the sales
culture was not an assertive, aggressive one. Management
decided that a new sales culture was called for. In this new arrangement, sales representatives were to be much more assertive—
identifying potential customers, making cold calls, calling current
customers to sell them new services, and being more assertive
in their sales routines. In fact, the new computer system was
designed, in part, to make the sales force more aggressive. The
consultants realized that this was largely countercultural. Therefore, in training people to use the new computer system, they
included a special program for the sales force, showing them
how to use the computer to conduct more assertive sales routines. The training program also highlighted the advantages of
being an assertive sales person. The compensation system was
changed to support the new sales culture, rewarding, in the beginning, a more assertive approach and moving later to a com-
mission approach. Even the shadow side of this compensation
program was discussed; while the company wanted its sales associates to do well, it did not want them shoving unneeded and
unwanted services down the throats of customers and in the
process alienating them.

The Stages of Model B

Model B is a comprehensive model for initiating and managing change. It adds functions, steps, or perspectives often missing in other models. The preferred scenario stage and integrating action into every stage and step of the model are examples of this.

A brief overview of each stage of Model B will give a better feeling for the entire process. This process need not be used in lockstep fashion. Like Models A and C, Model B is a tool or set of tools to help managers serve the business. In some cases it will make more sense to start with Stage Two or Stage Three instead of Stage One. Most managers move back and forth within the process as need arises.

Stage One: Current Scenario

Stage One is the assessment stage, the time to ask basic questions. What's going on? What are the issues that need attention? It has three distinct steps: (1) assessing deficits and identifying unused opportunities, (2) identifying blind spots and developing new perspectives, and (3) establishing change priorities and searching for points of leverage. Like the stages themselves, these steps are not necessarily carried out in the order in which they are presented here. And since planning without action is meaningless, discussion of how each of these steps is a stimulus to immediate action is provided.

Step One: Telling the Story. The basic question is, What are the critical issues in strategy, operations, structure, human resource management, management and supervision, and leadership? Note that Model A is used here as an assessment tool, a template that helps in a systematic way to identify areas needing attention, whether an outmoded strategy, an imperfect marketing plan, a structure that no longer serves the business, or a recruitment system that is not working. Model A, with its master tasks and subtasks, can be used to determine deficiencies and opportunities. Deficiency questions sound like this: What is going wrong? What are our weaknesses, faults, and deficiencies? What are we failing to do well? In what ways do we fall short of the exemplars in our field?

Since seizing opportunities often provides more leverage than merely correcting mistakes, there also is a set of opportunity-focused questions to be asked: What are our unused strengths? What challenges do we need to respond to? What opportunities have we been ignoring? In what ways could we be using our resources better? To what degree do we have the will to become a leader in our field? Even when there are glaring deficiencies, recasting them as challenges or opportunities helps create an upbeat climate for change. One retailer did an audit of its strategy as it was being played out in its stores. The audit firm returned from its investigation with some grim messages. At the meeting the president of the retailer said, "This is pure gold. We know that the strategy is not working the way we want it to work. Now we have some details that confirm our suspicions. This audit is a challenge."

A comprehensive audit produces the business, organizational, managerial, and leadership "story" of the company or institution. Consider the case of a foreign airline. In Step One the company first identified its deficits. "We have a range of business and organizational problems and many unused opportunities. For instance, a number of our top managers believe that selective markets and creative agreements with other carriers are the wave of the future. Trying to cover the entire globe, they say, makes the airline too vulnerable, especially when—and not if—deregulation, started in the United States, spreads to other countries. Some of our managers are convinced that our airline has to get out of the transportation business and into the service business, meaning that the airline needs to see itself as a service organization that happens to be in the transportation business. But many of our frontline people, those in direct contact with customers, lack both the skills and the authority needed to interact creatively with customers. Creative marketing and creative service are needed.

"Some of our problems and unused opportunities are internal, relating to the organization. For instance, a number of middle managers say that we have a performance appraisal system that is merely a ritual, in many ways an organizational joke. For a whole variety of reasons manager and supervisors either avoid writing the appraisals — over 50 percent are routinely late, some by as much as six months — or write perfunctory appraisals that help neither the company nor its employees. We have other internal problems: there are too many managerial layers, that is, the organization is too fat; too many top-level managers are without vision; career opportunities in terms of promotion have dried up; a significant number of middle managers are marking time until retirement; because of recent layoffs morale is low."

The company also identified some of its opportunities. "In spite of all this, there are many people, from top to bottom, who identify with the company and are eager to see it become one of the best airlines in the business. Our CEO has just announced a new vision and mission for the airline that appeals to them. And, although the history of the relationship between management and the unions has been a troubled one, there are indications that both sides are ready for a more creative partnership. The problem is that we are not currently leveraging these positive things."

This quick glance at the business and organizational problems and opportunities at the airline gives the gist of an assessment that includes both problems and at least some opportunities. The audit is probably too light on opportunities, and not enough of the problems have been recast as challenges. At any rate, the first step of Stage One is to know what is actually going on.

Sometimes the mere telling of the story is enough to galvanize a company or organizational unit into action. This is especially true in cases where the story has been covered up or has not been discussed in public forums within the system. Once the story is told, both the preferred scenario and some kind of action plan are clear. In such cases action rather than further planning is called for.

A consultant was asked to help a marketing team deal with some of its frustrations. During the first session, he helped the group uncover some of the covert group norms they found

least helpful. One such norm called for highly competitive behavior within the team. As one member put it, "We should be
competing with the marketing teams of the other companies in
the industry, not with one another." Merely naming and challenging this norm led to a more collegial spirit and many in-
stances of collaboration.

In the airline case, the word "fat" proved to be a catalyst.
Everyone knew that the airline would not compete unless it became lean. Some managers returned to their departments and
took an audit of the fat to be found there.

***Step Two: Identifying Blind Spots and Developing New Perspec-
tives.*** Companies, like people, develop blind spots. Questions
to be asked in Step Two are, What is *really* going on? What are
we overlooking? What's lurking in the shadows that keeps us
from getting ahead? While outside consultants can help organizations identify and deal with various forms of myopia, the
best organizations, realizing that blind spots, like rust, accumu-
late in the natural course of events and impair the effectiveness
of the system, build in self-monitoring systems. What are we
overlooking? should be an instinctive day-to-day question. But
even the best can be helped by objective outsiders who can help
identify and challenge blind spots.

In a more positive vein, Step Two also deals with developing new perspectives. Take the case of Corning Glass Works.
In the early 1980s, after thirteen years of growth, the consumer
products division of Corning began to stall. One reason for this
was a failure on the part of management to see the world as
it really was. First, lower-cost, high-quality, and more stylish
imports began to flood in from Japan and Taiwan. Second,
Corning managed to overlook one of the fastest-growing product
lines — microwave cookware. This market went from nothing
to $500 million almost overnight. To make matters worse, Corn-
ing's products were suitable for use in microwaves, but the company did not mount a campaign to let consumers know that until
early 1985. Only later did Corning get around to introducing
a specific microwave product line. Until 1984 Corning rarely
did market studies and rarely sampled consumer preferences.

The company was creating its own blind spots. Complacency in a turbulent environment breeds disaster. The company, like many others, discovered that it was much easier to lose market share than to get it back.

What we see here is the opposite of a culture of vigilance and how costly it is. Blind spots are often difficult to identify precisely because they are cultural in nature, rooted in covert assumptions, values, and norms that are both organizational and personal. The mere existence of blind spots does not imply ill will. Savvy individuals and organizations, realizing how universal it is to engage in self-deception as self-protection against painful truths, are more likely to engage in self-monitoring and even welcome painful, but useful, truths, whatever their source. Change and problem solving at their best involve the use of imagination. Identifying blind spots and developing new, more creative perspectives is an essential part of that process. Managers add value by challenging both their own blind spots and those of the organization itself.

Some managers ask, "If blind spots are, by definition, things we fail to see, how can we challenge our own?" Merely giving managers an opportunity to answer the question "What are we overlooking?" is enough to uncover many blind spots. The managers of one company, when challenged to explore their own blind spots, said, "While it is critical for us to get into new businesses in our industry, we have never been good at that. We're good at the tried and true. We have hired consultants who are no better at spotting new businesses than we are. In fact, we have become too dependent on inept consultants. We consistently misjudge markets and the marketing moves of our competitors. Furthermore, we overestimate the importance of our size and our technical skills. What we need is better management and marketing skills, and the truth is that we don't have them. We have always underestimated the need for flexibility and customer responsiveness. To make things worse, we don't learn from these mistakes. Finally, we try, we fail, and then we lose heart. When we lose heart, we fail to act decisively. For instance, once problems surface, we withhold capital investment from start-up ventures and allow them to wallow."

This is a case of business-enhancing honesty. Managing blind spots often means doing a very honest self-appraisal, no matter how much it hurts. Helping an organization identify its blind spots and develop new perspectives on problems and opportunities can trigger actions directly. For instance, a consultant helped a superintendent of a boys' reformatory who was desperate to improve the institution develop a whole new range of possibilities by changing from a custodial to an educational approach. Action started almost immediately. The best guards were trained in educational rather than custodial approaches, the best of these trained other guards, a merit system was installed in the cottages, and the boys were rewarded for learning. Within a year recidivism dropped almost 50 percent (see Carkhuff, 1974). Unfortunately, the politics of the institution and of the state in which it was located won out in the end, reversing all the gains made by these changes. Politics constituted a blind spot, it seems, for both the administrator and the consultants alike. They thought that good ideas that yield excellent results should win the day no matter what the political climate.

Step Three: Establishing Priorities and Searching for Points of Leverage. Learning the full story may reveal a whole range of business and organizational problems and opportunities. Or the problems and opportunities may be few but complex and far-reaching. Since everything cannot be done at once, it is essential that high-priority or value-added problems or opportunities be chosen for attention. Companies and institutions, once they have reviewed their operations and challenged blind spots, must ask themselves, What problems and opportunities, if addressed, will give us the greatest return on our investment? The issue is leverage. Which problems and which opportunities, if attended to, will move the company most quickly and substantively away from disaster and toward excellence?

Take the case of a large distributor of industrial products with a variety of business and organizational problems. The company developed and announced a new mission statement and strategy. Since it was essential to communicate the strategy to everyone in every unit of the company, it was seen as a golden opportunity to do something about the performance management system. This system, members of the change group believed, could be used as a primary tool for disseminating the strategy. One reason the company was adrift was its reliance on controls imposed by managers rather than controls embedded in the system and subscribed to by the workers themselves. The performance management system was a joke because it was not tied to effective planning and feedback. Since many people had vague objectives, received no feedback, and saw appraisal as a waste of time, pride in performance was, at best, a hit-and-miss affair.

Therefore, even though there were many other organizational problems, it was decided to reform this system because of its potential impact on everyone — a question of leverage. The company got rid of the formal language of performance management and renamed the system "The Energizer: How to Help People Give Their Best." Managers did not talk about setting objectives. Rather, in their dialogues with their direct reports, they asked, "What are the key things that need to be done around here?" Managers loved the new, no-nonsense system. They were encouraged, within commonsense guidelines, to tailor the system to their own units and involve everyone in the tailoring process. Then each manager had to tailor it to the specific needs of each direct report. Some workers were very good at coming up with creative, strategy-based objectives for themselves. Others needed to be walked carefully through the process. Still others needed to be assigned objectives and then discuss their contributions to the business. In sum, the company's decision to make the reformation of the performance management system a high priority paid off.

Choosing a "big ticket" problem or opportunity for attention can in itself stimulate action. "You're right! We've got the right strategy. We're headed in the right direction. But we don't have the right mix of products for the market niche we're trying to carve out." Statements such as these can lead to immediate action, at least lay the groundwork for the kind of action that gets the institution moving in the right direction.

In the case of the industrial products distributor, one of

the managers on the change task force, after listening to a consultant point out how useful and manager-friendly a performance management process could be, went out and did three things immediately. First, he tried the simple process the consultant had outlined with a number of his direct reports. Then he asked them, "What if we used this performance management process instead of the one we now have?" One of his direct reports replied, "I'd kiss your feet!" Second, he did an informal survey and sounded out about half a dozen other managers on the new process. All of them said, "This is so much better than what we now do. If we used this process, appraisals would be a snap." Finally, in a meeting with the president of the company, he shared the findings of his experiment and his survey. This was one of the most important factors in convincing the president to move forward with the new system.

The steps of Stage One are not limited to Stage One; significant facts concerning a company's "story" can emerge at any time during the change process. In one company, new facts about a competitor's market strategy were learned in the middle of a change effort. While this did not throw the process off course, significant adjustments had to be made. Furthermore, blind spots need to be identified and challenged throughout the change process. One hotel chain, after trying several ways of increasing profitability — including replacing a couple of key executives — without success, finally realized that the company was good at hotel management but not good at brick and mortar. They sold their properties on the condition that they receive long-term management contracts. Profitability increased significantly.

Finally, the need to assess and reassess change priorities in order to get the most leverage possible out of change efforts continues in Stages Two and Three. One manufacturing company was in the middle of designing a new structure when it became clear that lack of a customer relations program was a much more pressing problem. And so it put development of the new structure on hold. Once the customer relations program had been put in place, the company realized that it did not need a new structure. Modifications in the current structure were sufficient.

Stage Two: Preferred Scenario

While the work of Stage One is essential, the real power of Model B usually lies in the next two stages: developing preferred scenarios and finding ways of turning these scenarios into reality. These two steps are extremely important because they are about solutions or end states calling for imagination and creativity. They are dealt with in some detail elsewhere (Egan, 1988). The purpose here is to provide the reader with a feel for the nature and process of Model B rather than its details, so Stages Two and Three are outlined a bit more briefly than was Stage One.

Stage Two, in that it focuses on the development of a preferred scenario, is the heart of the change process. It is the point where imagination is most critical. Once the organization sees the deficit or the unused opportunity, the next step is not to look for ways of managing the problem or exploiting the opportunity, but rather to ask, What would the problem look like if managed? What would the opportunity look like if developed? What would be in place? What do we want the future to look like? Stage Two does not deal with solutions in terms of action strategies; it deals with solutions in terms of accomplishments, achievements, and outcomes. Many, if not most, approaches to change overlook this step and move from problem clarification to action-strategy solutions immediately. Stage Two is the pause that refreshes the imagination.

The Use of Model A in Stage Two

In Stage One, Model A is a template for assessment. The master tasks and subtasks are used to "take the pulse" of the company. In Stage Two, however, Model A, dealing as it does with the principles of business and organizational effectiveness, provides guidelines for developing the preferred scenario through its master tasks and subtasks. Change projects are exercises in redoing some part of strategy, operations, structure, human resource management systems, management/supervision systems, or the leadership system. For instance, in one company change revolved around strategy. Since Model A stresses the importance of cascading strategy throughout the organization and getting it to touch everything within the system, the preferred scenario included not just a picture of the strategy, but a picture of what the strategy would look like in every major department of the company. In another company, in which empire building within organizational units and lack of constructive interaction between the units was a problem, Model A was used to suggest remedies in terms of coordinating mechanisms, partnerships, interunit charters, and interunit teamwork.

The Steps of Stage Two

Stage Two has three steps: (1) developing a range of preferred scenarios for a better future, (2) crafting an "agenda" based on the range of possibilities, and (3) securing commitment from those who are to be responsible for bringing the preferred scenario on-line. As in Stage One, each of the steps is used as needed to add focus and definition to the change process.

Step One: Developing Preferred Scenario Possibilities. One school district, instead of starting a meeting of all its high school principals with a review of all the problems these schools faced, divided the principals into small groups and presented the following agenda: "Suppose that you were asked to develop from scratch the best high school in the United States. For the moment forget about the availability of the resources needed for this dream school. Rather, describe what it would look like in all its dimensions."

At the end of the morning each small group shared its "ten best" possibilities with the other groups. This proved to be one of the most exciting mornings in the history of the district. The principals went at the task tooth and nail. Many marveled at just how creative their colleagues could be.

In the afternoon, they were given a second task. The new question was, "How many of the preferred scenarios you brainstormed this morning could be put in place in your schools even with the resource constraints under which all of us are working?" The principals were amazed at how much they could do.

Realistic agendas were pieced together from modifications of what they had come up with in the morning. They went back to the same schools, but with a great deal more enthusiasm.

Step Two: Crafting an Agenda. Brainstorming preferred scenarios provides the building blocks for what will ultimately be a realistic, business-enhancing, preferred scenario. If a preferred scenario is to be realized, certain things must be done—there must be an agenda. The agenda for the preferred scenario should have the following characteristics. It should be

- Cast in outcome language—what should be in place
- Specific enough to drive action
- Challenging—capable of capturing the imagination of those who are to carry it out
- Realistic, even though people might have to stretch
- Substantial—it should have a real impact on the business
- Sustainable—the agenda should have staying power
- Flexible—it should be able to be adapted to a changing environment
- Compatible with the resources and culture of the business
- Cast in a reasonable time frame

Brainstorming can sometimes produce such a wealth of possibilities that it is difficult to choose among them. One troubled company was trying to decide on which of three possible marketing strategies to pursue. It was getting nowhere, however, because key stakeholders—the head of marketing, the head of sales, two board members, and a representative from a stockholders' group—could not resolve their differences. However, once they evaluated the alternatives objectively—in terms of the specificity, clarity, realism, adequacy, dynamism, cultural fit, degree of projected buy-in, projected financial consequences, and timeliness of these different marketing approaches—they had no difficulty making a choice. Making the choice created a "channel" of energy and action. Once everybody had bought into the new marketing agenda, they knew precisely what to do.

Step Three: Securing Commitment. As suggested in the sections dealing with the shadow side of change, identifying key stakeholders and getting them to buy into the change agenda right from the beginning is one critically important way of managing these shadow side realities. So it is assumed here that work has been going on throughout all the steps. At this point, however (that is, at the point where a definite change agenda has been established), it is essential to review what kind of commitment is needed from all players: What kind of commitment do we need from the financial community? What kind of commitment do we need from vendors? What kind of commitment do we need from buyers? What kind of commitment do we need from store managers? And so forth. Win-win partnerships need to be established.

Action Implications of Stage Two

Elaborating clear, realistic, imaginative, and compelling agendas lies at the heart of the process of organizational change. If the agenda has quality and appeal, then people will begin to work toward implementing it informally, even before the formal plan is in place. "What would your business look like if it were functioning like an industry leader?" can stimulate not only the imagination but also action. Indeed, some organizations need only this step. Once they spell out some of the details of the future they want, they know how to get there. A principal who had attended the workshop mentioned earlier went back to her school, set up a meeting with some of the parents who had shown willingness to get actively involved in the school, designed a parent participation program with them, and had a pilot up and running within a week.

Stage Three: Strategy

Many models of change ask two basic questions: What's going wrong? How do we fix it? Since Model B adds an in-between stage — What do we really want? — the question in Stage Three is not How do we fix it? but rather How do we get from the current to the preferred scenario? Stage Three is about creative ways of "getting there." There are several critical questions to be asked at this stage: How do we get from here to there? Who is going to do what and when? How can commitment to the change venture be sustained?

Sometimes the answers to these questions will be quite clear. At other times they will demand a great deal of searching. The overarching question is, How do we make sure that the actions we are planning will lead to the desired outcomes we have identified and committed ourselves to? Stage Three has three distinct steps: (1) brainstorming possible strategies for bringing the preferred scenario on-line, (2) choosing a best-fit package of high-leverage or value-added strategies, and (3) formulating an implementation plan based on these best-fit strategies.

Step One: Brainstorming Strategies. Many different questions can be used to stimulate thinking about paths to preferred goals: What should we do? How do we get there? How many ways can we accomplish our goals? What can we do right away? What do we need to do later? Who should do what? How do we get started? What are the principal routes to our destination? It is not always easy to get managers to do this kind of brainstorming. Yet, failure to brainstorm can lead to disastrous results. Consider these two cases.

- *The disadvantage of the single-strategy approach.* A large chemical company instituted an early retirement scheme to trim down the organization by some five thousand people. However, more than twice the anticipated number of employees took advantage of the scheme. The result? The company had to hire back many of the retirees as consultants at hefty salaries. The process cost them more than if they had done nothing.
- *The advantage of brainstorming a range of strategies.* A major airline knew that it would have to downsize after a merger with a smaller airline. The company wanted to drop about two thousand people, but also wanted to retain key people. Therefore, it brainstormed not only ways of downsizing but also ways of

retaining the best; members of the human resource department came up with more than thirty action strategies to achieve each of these outcomes. Not only did they lose the kind of people they wanted to, but there were no strikes and very little organizational disruption.

I asked a group of managers who had developed an excellent agenda for change to brainstorm ways of accomplishing this agenda. They wanted to quit after identifying two or three strategies. After much coercion on my part, they came up with about fifteen action strategies in all. Then, in line with the second task of Stage Three, I asked them to choose the best strategies from among the fifteen. After much discussion, they chose strategies one, seven, and fourteen. Their choices made it clear that, had they not brainstormed, they would have missed two of the best strategies. As the story shows, there is no such thing as the "one right strategy." Premature closure in considering possible strategies for achieving the preferred scenario is one of the major pitfalls in change efforts.

Step Two: Choosing the Best Strategies. Highly creative implementation strategies are never good in and of themselves. They are useless unless they can be tailored to fit available resources and the prevalent culture. To improve the performance of managers, one company purchased an off-the-shelf management development program from a nationally known consulting and training firm. In the end, it was too expensive, it was too didactic for the company's action-oriented managers, it distracted them from day-to-day problems, and it promoted skills and methods that did not fit the company's culture. Managers found excuses for not attending training sessions, and the program died a quiet, if costly, death. Two years later, a consultant who had been helping line managers deal with a wide range of business issues got together with an internal committee and put together a simple, first-step management development program. This new program was based on the assumption that everyone was to participate in self-development and that all managers would be developers of people. The program was designed to meet immediate business needs. That program is still in place and has grown gradually. Line managers run many of the training sessions. It is adding value rather than cost.

Step Three: Formulating a Plan. Finally, once a set of best-fit strategies has been chosen, the purpose of Step Three is to mold best-fit strategies into viable plans. An implementation plan is a step-by-step outline of actions to be taken to achieve some valued outcome. At their best, plans are incentives to action and ways of making time a friend rather than an enemy of change.

Chaos was rampant at a start-up software company. The business had some excellent products and the money was rolling in, but there was little planning for anything. After two years, the founder-CEO had the sense to replace himself with a president with a great deal of business acumen. The founder moved into the newly created post of chairman, but his love was still new-product development. The president's job was to bring order to the chaos without infringing on the entrepreneurial spirit that drove the company. He started by tightening up accounting procedures but then moved quickly to change the company's haphazard approach to marketing. With the help of a consultant and with input from the chairman and two people who had been with the company from the start, he put together a new marketing strategy. Coming up with a plan to make the new strategy work was another thing. He put together a marketing strategy implementation task force and included one hotshot programmer.

Next, the president wrote on pieces of cardboard the components of the current hit-and-miss approach to marketing and put them up on the conference room wall at different angles and in no particular order. When the task force met, the president first gave a brief, clear presentation of the highlights of the new marketing strategy. Then, counting on the programming instincts of the group, he asked the task force members to rearrange the pieces on the wall in whatever order they thought would produce results. He told them to get rid of pieces that were no longer needed and to add pieces that were missing. He provided them with a stack of blank pieces of cardboard and left the room. He came back an hour or so later and there, arranged in apple-pie order, was the plan for the rollout of the new marketing strategy. And it was the employees' plan. They told him to call on them if he needed more help in getting things organized.

Action Implications of Stage Three

Any or all the steps of Stage Three can stimulate immediate action. Brainstorming possible strategies can lead to pilot programs. Choosing a package of best-fit strategies can get managers to choose a couple of people to champion the change agenda in their departments. Announcing an action plan can turn fence sitters into doers. One company was dragging its feet on closing a plant because of the agony involved in such a process. A manager from a different plant attended a seminar on "cutting back" and as a follow-up to the seminar visited a plant belonging to another company that was in the process of closing. He saw a very well defined closing plan in action. He volunteered to act as a consultant to the manager of the plant to be closed. Sharing some of the strategies he saw being used successfully in the other company served as the trigger for action. The plant was closed within a year.

The new manager of a training division of a midsize company inherited a management trainer who did not meet her expectations in terms of both competency and team participation. Her goal was to have a trainer in place who could train effectively and work well with the rest of the team. She had several options with respect to the nonperformer: develop him, fire him, work for his transfer elsewhere in the personnel department, give him simple administrative duties in the training unit, help him find work in a subsidiary, help him find work outside the company, use him in training programs with nonmanagerial staff, or create a new job for him within the unit, such as audio-visual coordinator or director of a management development resource facility. Two facts influenced the manager's decision. First, her preferred agenda was to have an effective management trainer in place. Second, the manager discovered that the trainer in question, who had always been known as a loner, was talking down the training unit around the organization.

The manager chose the option of helping the trainer get a job in another company and thereby opened the position for a high-quality trainer. This helped morale in the training unit. The manager started work on hiring a new trainer immediately and found a replacement within three months. The culture of this company included a covert norm of keeping incompetent employees, provided they not cause "trouble." In fact, they caused plenty of trouble by limiting the firm's productivity and causing resentment among productive workers. Firmly choosing a strategy precipitated action in the human resources department.

Figure 7.2 presents a visual summary of the stages and steps involved in Model B.

From Planning to Execution

In effective change programs, outcome-producing action, as has been emphasized over and over, starts from the very beginning

Figure 7.2. The Stages of Model B.

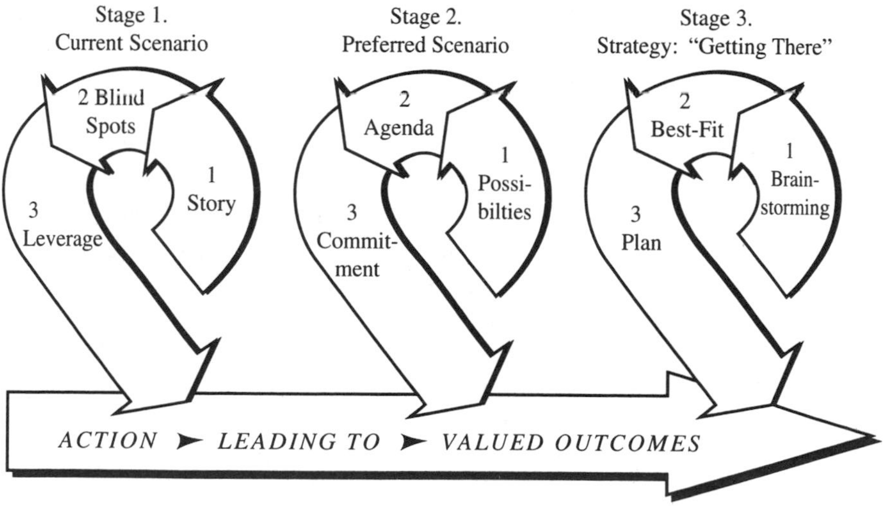

ACTION ▶ LEADING TO ▶ VALUED OUTCOMES

of the project and continues throughout. These "little" actions during the diagnosis and planning process constitute one of the best signs of the organization's commitment to change. However, once a formal plan has been drawn up, the formal transition phase begins, that is, the transition from the current to the preferred scenario. Effective leaders not only turn visions into realistic agendas and arouse enthusiasm for these agendas by the very way in which they communicate them to others but also foment problem solving and learning around these agendas and make sure that organizational actors persist until the agendas are accomplished. In many ways the transition phase is about tactics and logistics. Tactics is the art of being able to adapt a plan to the immediate situation; it is the art of persistence. Logistics is the art of getting the right resources to the right place at the right time.

In the execution phase the shadow side of planning gives way to the equally virulent shadow side of implementation. Once more, forewarned is forearmed.

The Shadow Side Revisited

The formal transition phase is a critical time when many things can go wrong. Three common problems during this phase are overload, inertia, and entropy.

Overload

In change projects, people must get the day-to-day work of the system done and at the same time carry out the action strategies that lead to implementation of the preferred scenario. Overload is part of the shadow side of change; the time demands of the change project often are not coordinated with normal work schedules. When workers, even those committed to the goals of some change project, are given too much to do, they will either let their current work suffer or they will fail to implement their part of the change effort.

In one company a task force was dealing with a substantive change program. The president noticed that one of the task force team leaders was missing. He remarked that the team leader evidently was "not interested in change" and muttered something about replacing him. The truth is, that man's boss, fearing the changes that were about to take place, gave him so many assignments that he simply could not get to the meeting.

Very often, if forced to make a choice, workers will continue to meet day-to-day operational deadlines and give short shrift to the change project. Asking people to stretch to meet new goals is one thing. Asking them to do the impossible is another.

Inertia

Two principal enemies of action are inertia and entropy. Inertia is the opposite of get-up-and-go. It is the kind of sit-down-and-stop that plagues many change efforts. Many good ideas and plans never get off the ground.

Consider the case of a thirteen-hospital health care system. The administrator and the members of the board discussed possible changes in the policies and procedures of the system. It soon became evident to a consultant sitting in on the meeting that the administrator ran the show with a rather heavy hand. When asked if the company had ever engaged in similar exercises, the administrator opened one of the drawers of her desk, pulled out a forbiddingly thick tome, set it on the desk in front of her, and said, "Oh, certainly. There was a group of consultants here just over a year ago. Here is the final report. I must admit, however, that we've been extremely busy and haven't had a chance to do much about its recommendations."

So much for organizational readiness for change and the "power" of a formal change plan. But this is hardly an isolated instance. The number of unimplemented change plans in desk drawers is legion.

The main reason plans do not work is that they are never really tried. Obviously the administrator had been opposed to the project from the very beginning. Dragging her feet was enough to prevent any serious push to implement the recommendations. Poorly conceived change projects deserve inertia,

but even good ones, as Hamlet said, "lose the name of action."
What is often called for in organizational change is a "dialogue"
between planning and action. Weick (1979) went so far as to
suggest that "chaotic action is preferable to orderly inaction":

> Action, when viewed retrospectively, clarifies what
> the organization is doing, what business it is in,
> and what its projects may be. Inaction, viewed
> retrospectively, is more puzzling and more sense-
> less: there is a greater likelihood for bizarre mean-
> ings to be attached and for an unhealthy amount
> of autism to be introduced. Action, in other words,
> provides tangible items that can be attended to. . . .
> Thus, when there is confusion and some member
> of a group asks, "What should I do?" and some other
> member says, "I don't know, just do something,"
> that's probably a much better piece of advice than
> you might realize. It's better for the simple reason
> that it increases the likelihood that something will
> be generated which can then be made meaningful
> (pp. 245–246).

Weick did not suggest that chaotic activity is best. However,
it is certainly better than the endless talking and planning for
change that promises much but delivers little.

The three stages of Model B constitute planning for action, not action itself. Indeed, in many companies and institutions overplanning is the principal form of inertia. People talk
endlessly about what needs to be done and different ways of doing it. In such cases, each of the stages of Model B should be
renamed "blah," thus turning planning into a lot of "blah, blah,
blah."

Entropy

Entropy is the tendency of things human to fall apart. To understand the major problems of the transition phase, most of
us need only reflect on our own experiences in trying to imple-

ment personal plans. The plans we make seem realistic to us. We launch into the initial steps with a good deal of enthusiasm. However, we soon run into tedium, obstacles, and complications. What seemed so easy in the planning stage now seems quite difficult. We become discouraged, flounder, recover, flounder again, and finally give up, offering ourselves rationalizations as to why we did not want to accomplish those goals anyway.

Overload, inertia, and entropy do not necessarily signal ill will on the part of managers or workers. Rather they are part of life. If we do not control them, they will control us. Both individuals and social systems are often at risk during the transition state. During the action or transition phase, organizations need to let go of one trapeze bar, that is, familiar but unproductive patterns of behavior, and grab hold of a new one, new and more productive patterns of behavior.

A culture of vigilance is the first-line defense against overload, inertia, and entropy. In change efforts there are at least two kinds of vigilance: initial vigilance that signals the need for change in the first place and follow-up vigilance. Follow-up vigilance focuses on whatever prevents even good plans from getting off the ground and on whatever tends to make even robust change efforts fall apart over time.

In sum, then, if initiating and managing change is a key managerial responsibility, then managers should have a shared model of change that provides them with a methodology for dealing with change and a language for talking about change.

EIGHT

Creating a Preferred Culture: The Learning Organization

In Chapter Six it was suggested that one of the key roles of the manager is to develop, maintain, and reinforce a preferred culture. The paradigm of the learning organization provides an excellent substrate or culture for the models of management outlined in this book. A learning organization culture means "What we do around here is learn; we learn continuously and use our learning to improve everything we do." The purpose of this chapter is (1) to pull together the current business and organizational effectiveness paradigms that are related to the learning organization concept, including such approaches as total quality management and "constant incremental improvement," and (2) to show how managers can use these paradigms to create a preferred learning organization culture that serves the business.

The term *learning* in this context has a decidedly pragmatic flavor. Business applications rather than theory is the focus. Here, then, *pragmatic learning* implies that learning takes place when value-added options are discovered and implemented. Pragmatic learning focuses on increasing business-enhancing options. Increased options are important because, other things being equal, better decisions are made when decision makers can choose from among alternatives. A company in a learning mode is constantly looking for value-added options, for instance, unexploited niches for its products. It develops a "culture of vigilance" that enables it to identify such opportunities.

Companies often lock themselves into a narrow range of options. Unfortunately, companies, like people, do not instinctively search for more productive options. A company with a single product operating in a single market niche is at risk in a highly competitive environment. Competitors might come along with new products, better products, or lower-cost products or merely take the niche away with greater marketing power and prowess. When a company asks itself, What do we need to do in order to thrive rather than merely survive? it enters a learning mode, that is, it begins the search for options. For a company or institution, learning means increasing the system's options in key business, organizational, and managerial areas. These options, once exploited, lead to increased productivity and quality of work life.

An Advanced Organizer: What Chapter Eight Is About

- *Metaphors for a Learning Organization.* Thinking about organizations as living organisms and as brains provides a foundation for creating a learning organization culture.
- *Developing a Learning Organization Culture.* Although each company has to develop its own learning organization culture, there are many useful building blocks available, including systems thinking, Senge's "five disciplines," planning as learning, total quality management programs, constant improvement and employee involvement programs, benchmarking, and learning from change.
- *The Stages of a Learning Organization.* Learning organizations move from increased efficiency to improved effectiveness and on to transformation.
- *Competencies Needed in a Learning Organization.* Learning organizations have some basic competencies, including anticipatory learning, double-loop learning, learning through debate, learning through risk taking, learning from noxiants, and learning from mistakes.
- *The Shadow Side of a Learning Organization.* These pitfalls in-

clude fad, the name itself, cynicism about culture change, organizational learning disabilities, defensive routines, and overcontrol.

The term *learning organization* has been knocking around for a while. For instance, in 1988 Hayes, Wheelwright, and Clark used the term in a book on manufacturing excellence. They claimed that one of the critical success factors in high-performance plants is the ability to learn and to use learning to improve performance over the long haul. The concept of the learning organization continues to develop. It has become popular in describing companies and institutions that have committed themselves to a culture of constant improvement. Managers of these institutions, keenly aware of the turbulent environments in which they operate, realize that the only way they will stay even with or, better, get ahead of competition is to learn how to do things better. The learning curve involves some mix of improving current ways of doing things and finding better ways. For instance, chemical companies must constantly improve their manufacturing processes and lower their costs in doing so, but they must also come up with new products that better meet the needs of their customers and the needs of the environment.

There is no one right way of becoming a learning organization. Each company has to review the various ways of becoming a learning organization and choose those that best fit its character. Learning in the sense of developing value-added options is needed in every master task and subtask of Model A. Ray Stata (1989), the chairman of Analog Devices, a strong proponent of a learning organization culture, claimed that in the United States the lack of innovation in management is a more serious problem than lack of technology and product innovation. Managerial learning, then, can be the key to increased options because it is intimately linked to every other kind of learning.

Metaphors for a Learning Organization

In his book *Images of Organization,* Gareth Morgan (1986) discusses eight metaphors that help us think creatively about organizations. Two of these have a special relationship to the learning organization: organizations as organisms and organizations as brains.

The Organism Metaphor: Open-Systems Learning

Companies and institutions are open systems—living organisms, as it were—in an ever-changing environment. In turbulent times it is important for institutions to learn from their environments and adapt to them. In relatively stable environments where market conditions are well understood, manufacturers can focus on such things as improving the efficiency of production. On the other hand, in highly volatile and unpredictable environments in which technological advances are fast and furious and in which there are boundless market opportunities together with market "black holes"—the environment in which computer and automobile companies currently operate—enterprises must remain on an incessant and often steep learning curve. They must constantly learn how to develop and use new technology and stay abreast of fast-moving market conditions. The more turbulent the environment, the more open these firms must be to learning from the environment and the more quickly they must gear the organization of work, the nature of authority and decision making, communication systems, and employee involvement to constantly evolving conditions. As we approach the twenty-first century, more and more companies and institutions are moving toward the "need to adapt" philosophy because economic, political, social, and industry environments have become more and more turbulent. For instance, the paradoxical inability of many educational systems to learn to adapt to economic, political, and social turbulence has led to an unparalleled crisis in education in the United States.

The Brain Metaphor: Everyone a Learner

The brain has an amazing ability to continue to function as a whole even when parts of it are incapacitated. It is as if the whole of the brain were involved in almost everything it does. Because of this versatility and flexibility, the "brain offers itself as an obvious metaphor for organization, particularly if our concern is to improve capacities for organizational intelligence" (Morgan, 1986, p. 79). In these days when employee involvement programs are in full swing in many companies, it no longer makes sense to see just the top management team as the "brains" of the organization, with everyone else part of the "machine." The search for excellence and the pursuit of quality demand that every worker — or at least a critical mass of workers — be in a learning mode. The time has come "to think of organizations as if *they were brains,* and to see if we can create forms of organization that disperse brainlike capacities throughout an enterprise" (p. 79, italics in original). Organizations that are too dependent on the thinking of one person or even one small group of persons run the risk of being less than they could be, because of failure to tap into the intellectual resources and wisdom that are spread throughout the institution.

Moving Beyond Bounded Rationality

While there is no one right way to learn, these two metaphors and the approaches to learning that are discussed in this chapter all imply moving beyond what Morgan called *bounded rationality,* which is often defined by the old, play-it-safe culture. In learning organizations creative thinking and intuition serve the institution. Research on right-brain versus left-brain functions suggests that the two can complement each other. Many companies and institutions have traditionally undervalued the "holistic, analogical, intuitive, and creative capacities of the brain's right hemisphere" (pp. 107–108). Some institutions have made the mistake of trying to rectify this imbalance by moving far along the continuum to a more radical right-brain approach. Some kind of balance is called for, different in different companies. One energy company, for instance, established an in-house think tank. Ideas flowed freely in what some dubbed the "playpen," but these ideas were let out into the mainstream only when their business value — at a reasonable level of risk — was determined.

Many managers say they do not have enough time to "think about the business." They read very little and tend to discount ideas that do not emerge immediately from a business setting. However, many of them when dragged, sometimes kicking and screaming, through a business-related brainstorming session, have a change in heart. They begin to value good ideas no matter what their origin and they become more willing to blend "blue sky" thinking with hard-nosed analysis.

Developing a Learning Organization Culture

A wide range of methods for improving both business and the organization that is to serve it have been developed over the past few years. They can serve as building blocks for creating a learning organization culture. While each method is often presented as the "means of salvation," they are actually learning approaches that require a great deal of planning, commitment, and work. They are not formulas. They are not magic.

What is presented here is a "taste" of each of these frameworks or models. To get the full flavor, you can consult the original sources. Perhaps the first step, after reading this chapter, is to do a learning organization audit. The first question is, Now that we see, from a number of different perspectives, what is meant by a learning organization, what are our current strengths and weaknesses as a learning organization? Question two is, What approaches to learning make sense for us? The third question asks, How can we integrate these approaches into a tailored framework that will promote the kind of learning we need?

The methods considered in this chapter are systems thinking, Senge's "five disciplines," planning as learning, total quality management (TQM), constant improvement and employee involvement programs, benchmarking, and learning from change. Each in its own way helps to develop a learning organization.

Systems Thinking

The members of effective learning teams see the interconnectedness of things. Actions often reverberate throughout the organization in terms of unintended effects. For instance, one company changed its structure but did not foresee the ways in which the new structure would inhibit its ability to implement its strategy. In another company the transfer of a manager who was about to champion a new project made the host department scrap the project and return to the drawing board. In still another a delay in the introduction of a new product caused inventory problems. In the same company new computer-based credit procedures led to problems in cash flow.

People too often focus on isolated parts or activities of a system. The systems thinker automatically asks, What will the reverberations of this be? Systems thinking helps team members see patterns and act to reinforce them if they are system-enhancing or change them if they are system-limiting. Model A, as noted earlier, promotes systems thinking among managers. And since it deals with stakeholders and the environment, the system in question is not limited to the company or institution itself.

Both individuals and institutions get trapped into narrow, provincial modes of thinking — about themselves, about the business, and about the world in which they live. Becoming a learning organization involves thinking more broadly about strategy, operations, structure, human resource management systems, supervisory and managerial practice, and leadership. Railroads have been cited as the classic example. They saw themselves as railroads rather than transportation companies. If they had thought of themselves and the world more broadly, we might now be flying the New York Central Airline. On the other hand, the fortunes of Scandinavian Airlines began to turn around when the company decided to see itself as a service company that happened to be in the transportation business.

Joseph McCann (1991), a member of Egon Zehnder International, a consulting firm, has outlined seven kinds of interrelated and overlapping thinking that are needed to help fashion a learning organization. Each involves a paradigm shift, "a fundamental change in the way we view the world and in how individuals, groups, and organizations relate to each other" (p. 77). A word on each — but first a caution. Moving to a new paradigm does not necessarily mean casting the old paradigm aside completely, because the old paradigm may still have its uses. If the new paradigm is long-term thinking, there are still times when short-term thinking is required. It is often more a case of getting the right blend of paradigms than leaving the old one behind completely. McCann claimed that many, if not most, companies and institutions come up short on the following kinds of systems thinking:

Organic Thinking. This involves a shift from "machine" to systems thinking. Neither the world nor the companies and institutions within it are machines; they are systems. Organic thinking emphasizes context and relationships. The skills of synthesis must complement the skills of analysis. These are dynamic rather than static. Companies that think organically, since they appreciate complexity, avoid the "one right answer" trap. They explore multiple routes to ever-shifting goals. They prize flexibility and adaptability. Pepsico remains successful because it creates markets and products when it can, adapts to market realities when this is the road to success, and knows when to do each. It is a vital company. Companies that think organically know that survival is the issue. The steel industry in the United States seemed headed for disaster, but from the debacle emerged the highly successful minimills. Creativity, adaptability, and flexibility are part of their vitality.

Pluralistic Thinking. Companies and institutions are open systems, affected daily by environmental events, not tightly bound entities unto themselves. Key environmental events are not outside; they are living within and affecting the business. The skin of an organization is more like a sieve than an iron jacket. Companies thinking pluralistically do not formulate strategies without thinking of the impact of stakeholders on the system. Management, employees, government regulatory bodies, the communities in which business is transacted, suppliers, customers, lenders, shareholders, environmental groups, and others all have a "stake" in the business. These stakes change over time and need to be factored into the formulation of strategy. IBM has been fashioning a strategy that requires a leaner workforce, fewer suppliers, a different distribution system, and greater responsiveness to customer needs. The computer giant has become painfully aware of the ways it has failed to deal with a pluralistic world, one in which competitors do not follow IBM formulas, and is trying to find its way again. Industry analysts are not sure how successful the company will be in repositioning itself.

Process Thinking. Thinking in terms of structures is static; thinking in terms of value-added work flow is dynamic. Many companies operate in an economy where speed to market is critical. This is impossible when static hierarchical and bureaucratic concerns take precedence over dynamic business concerns. Ideally, companies create structures to channel business-enhancing work flow. A fair number of companies change structures quite frequently, but not all these changes serve the business. Some companies with business problems hope that changing the structure — moving the boxes around on the organizational chart — will improve the business. They are whistling in the wind. They need to find business solutions to business problems. A new structure will not salvage a bad strategy. On the other hand, some companies change organizational structures frequently because they need fluid structures to respond quickly to changes in the business environment. IBM has been hamstrung by its bureaucracy. Smaller, more fleet-of-foot enterprises have stolen their thunder, for instance in the laptop and now in the notebook computer markets. Often by the time the giant catches up, technology has taken the market elsewhere.

Pulse Thinking. *Pulse thinking* is the opposite of program thinking. The term comes from the image of blood pulsating through the arteries. Pulse thinking is not tied down to stages and steps; rather, it focuses on continuous flow. At one time companies could take their time in drawing up sophisticated plans and then implement them stage by stage. The company was in charge. Now the business environment and the marketplace are in charge. Japanese automobile makers and electronics firms have changed their industries forever. They "pulse" new products into the marketplace whenever they are ready. U.S. manufacturers are fighting to cut down the time from car conception to delivery, but they are playing catch-up with the Japanese. The "from conception to design to engineering to manufacturing to marketing to sales" step-and-stage approach is a form of program thinking that is no longer viable. All the key players involved with the ultimate launch of a new car must be involved from the first moment. And the sacred unveilings of new models in the fall are a thing of the past. New models hit the showrooms when they are available. Sony and Canon, for example, have become very sophisticated in a range of interrelated technologies, such as miniaturization and optics, which have allowed them to "pulse" out an amazing number of products to meet customers' apparent needs.

Another form of pulse thinking that moves away from discrete steps to continuous flow is *fuzzy logic*. This was just an odd mathematical idea a few years ago. But it allows computers to think, not just in terms of yes and no, but also maybe, sort of, and to a degree. The concept was developed in the United States. Today Japanese manufacturers use it to make elevators and washing machines work more smoothly and to allow air conditioners to adapt to weather conditions more efficiently. In summary, companies with an outmoded "program" mentality need to balance their approach to business with more pulse thinking.

National/Global Thinking. Narrow regional thinking is no longer enough. The global village is upon us, not just in an information-dispensing media sense, but in terms of the marketplace. In the petrochemical industry, it is believed that it is now impossible to be a substantive player without being a serious global player—not just an exporter, but a company with manufacturing capability in key parts of the world, a company that knows how to establish strategic alliances across the world and make them work. Many businesses, then, do not have a choice. They go global or they wallow and die. As McCann has well noted, given the right climate, technological innovations can emerge anywhere in the world: "There are many new technologies which simply do not have national allegiances" (p. 82). Biotechnology is one of them, with India having the capability of becoming a major player. In many businesses, being a nationwide or international player lends credibility in local markets.

Partnership Thinking. There has been an explosion in the rate at which companies are entering into alliances and partnerships, at times even with competitors. It is hard to open the *Wall Street Journal* on any given day without finding an announcement of a new partnership such as IBM and Apple. Indeed, a "go it alone at all costs" mentality may be the road to decline, if not disaster. The opportunities of win-win partnerships are seemingly endless. Win-win partnerships demand new skills, especially negotiation and conflict management skills. Managers used to having their own way and companies with an "I win, you lose" approach to the marketplace need to change focus or at least come up with a better balance. Recently British Airways announced its intention to establish a partnership with USAir. This sent shockwaves through the industry because, for all practical purposes, the new entity would become the fourth U.S. megacarrier, after American, Delta, and United. Since its privatization, British Airways has constantly taken a global systems perspective. Currently it is one of the most profitable of the large airlines.

Long-Term Thinking. Many industry observers analyze and criticize the factors that lock U.S. managers into short-term thinking. Wall Street is blamed for overemphasizing quarterly financial results. Senior managers, being older, play it safe on their watch — "no disasters here before my retirement." Recently ICI, the British chemical giant, pulled back from its high-performance plastics business. Industry analysts believe that someday this will be a very profitable business, but in the current development stage it is cash-hungry. Some say that the Japanese will take the long view, provide the cash, and end up owning the business. Managers cannot think long term if they are swamped by current operations. Thinking long term means climbing a hill, looking around, and stretching to look beyond the horizon. In societies that emphasize immediate results and gratification, this is difficult to do.

The Five Disciplines of a Learning Organization

Peter Senge (1990a, 1990b) is one of the current leaders in thinking and writing about the learning organization. According to

Senge, managers need to become both *adaptive learners,* that is, they must learn how to cope, and *generative learners,* that is, they must learn how to innovate. In many ways the successful Ford Taurus was a product of adaptive learning. It was a question of catching up with the Japanese. The Mazda Miata, on the other hand, was a product of generative learning: "It required a leap of imagination to see what the customer might want" (Senge, 1990b, p. 8). According to Senge, managers must continually practice and get better at five "disciplines": personal mastery, breaking away from limiting mental models, building a shared vision, learning as a team, and, as already seen, systems thinking. In fact, systems thinking is "the fifth discipline," which gives Senge's book its name. The need for systems thinking has already been outlined; here is a word about the other four.

Personal Mastery. The focus here is on the individual as learner. Senge called this commitment to personal mastery the learning organization's "spiritual foundation." At one company, "Everyone a learner, everyone into self-development first" is the motto of the "people development" program. Personal mastery, the enemy of mediocrity, is a prerequisite for team participation. It includes an institution-compatible personal vision, the use of the creative tension generated from falling short of the vision, and a relentless commitment to uncover self-limiting practices and modes of self-deception.

Breaking Away from Limiting Mental Models. People, deep down, often harbor mental models of the way things are or the way they believe things should be done. These mental models limit creativity and, as we have seen, are part of the shadow side of the organization. Managers committed to learning ferret out such "stinkin' thinkin'" and open it up to public challenge and disconfirmation. In one company a new team member admitted that he had gotten used to working from a political rather than a productivity model. He engaged in activities that scored points rather than increased productivity. He asked the members of the team to help him monitor his behavior. General Motors managers held company-limiting mental models that they began to exorcise only when forced to do so by the Japanese.

One of those was, "Cars are primarily status symbols. Styling is therefore more important than quality." The rest, as they say, is history. Amoco Chemical Company managers ferreted out the "paradigms" that kept it from preeminence and got down to work ridding itself of them.

Building a Shared Vision. While senior managers of a company or institution may play a key role in formulating and disseminating an overall vision, these visions must be translated into business reality by everyone else. Mere compliance is not enough. In light of the overall vision, managers need to develop "pictures of the future" to which they can commit themselves. In one company, the CEO's vision was uninspiring. Most accused him of dreaming. However, there was not much of a team spirit in the company and little was done to reach out and embrace the vision or even a scaled-down version of it. Model A highlights the importance of vision in formulating strategy. Model B emphasizes the importance of vision in creating the preferred scenario.

Learning as a Team. Senge sees teams rather than individuals as the basic learning units in a company or institution. Certainly, individual members must work at personal mastery, as outlined above, but learning as a team is a prerequisite. The most productive learning is team learning. This means that team members have to overcome defensiveness and communicate clearly and openly with one another. A member of one of the merchandising teams of a large retailer said of her experience one year, "I've never felt so exposed and I've never learned so much." Arie de Geus (1988), the former head of planning at Royal Dutch/Shell, noted that titmice, smaller, long-tailed songbirds that travel in flocks and mix freely with one another, quickly learned how to pierce the seals on milk bottles left on doorsteps. Robins, on the other hand, being territorial and antagonistic communicators, do not benefit from shared learning. Individual robins learned how to pierce the seals, but not robins as a group. According to de Geus, "the best learning takes place in teams that accept that the whole is larger than the sum of the parts, that there is a good that transcends the individual" (p. 74). The most successful companies develop teams of people who trust one another, complement one another's strengths, compensate for one another's weaknesses, aim for goals beyond any given individual's aspirations, and produce results that are consistently beyond the ordinary. The team IQ, for all practical purposes, is far greater than the IQ of any member. Team members are committed to continual improvement, discard preconceived notions as to what can be accomplished, and share a vision of success. Model A focuses on the need for both interunit and intraunit teamwork.

Admittedly, there is an idealistic flavor about Senge's writings. There is something heroic about the individual committed to personal mastery, the focused team, and the learning organization. On the other hand, as noted in Chapter One, companies that lack these characteristics have a great deal of unused potential. It might not take much to get them to make dramatic progress. Shared models of managing and leading are ways of making companies and institutions move ahead dramatically. At least, as the quality movement has demonstrated, it is possible.

Planning as Learning

Planning is a third possible building block of a learning organization, because planning at its best is about learning. It is a process of discovery, a search for options. Strategic planning at Analog Devices is a case in point. The company used the planning process as an opportunity for systemwide learning. The highly decentralized company formed fifteen corporatewide product, market, and technology task forces consisting of some 150 professionals across the company in order to understand and take advantage of the opportunities the company faced as a corporation. The company knew a great deal about the opportunities facing each division but did not know nearly enough about synergies among the divisions. The company learned that its almost fanatical commitment to decentralization was impeding progress. As a result, senior managers decided to coordinate technology development across divisions and to centralize certain aspects of manufacturing, especially wafer fabrication. In many companies planning is a sterile exercise, one often relegated to staff units. Analog Devices used planning as a way of changing minds and not just setting goals. De Geus, mentioned earlier, was an ardent proponent of planning as learning. He saw it as a way of getting inside the thinking that goes on within the company itself, in the marketplace, and within competitors. Planners at their best are challengers, facilitators, catalysts, accelerators, and goads for business-enhancing learning. One oil industry leader has said that de Geus's goading was not always appreciated by Shell's managers and that some of his approaches constituted overkill. But he did influence the company to move toward a learning organization paradigm. Model A, in that it promotes strategic and operational planning, and Model B, as a planning-for-change process, are tools of discovery and therefore tools of learning.

Total Quality Management Programs

Total quality management programs are a fourth possible learning organization building block. As noted in Chapter One, quality, in its narrow sense, is an aspect or dimension of a product or service. And so BMW produces "quality" automobiles, the Four Seasons Hotels provides "quality" guest accommodations, and the Cathedral in Oakland provides "quality" liturgy. However, if quality means not just meeting high standards but meeting both internal and external customers' expressed requirements, meeting customers' latent needs or requirements, exceeding customers' expectations, doing things right the first time, and continually accelerating the quality improvement process, then quality is a process that must affect every key program and activity within a company or institution. This is the "total" in total quality management. A quality strategy must drive a quality set of operations; a quality structure and a quality package of human resource management systems must serve the business; quality supervision, management, and leadership must make all this happen.

Quality in this broad sense is not a goal but an unending

quest. Everything can always be done better; quality can always be improved. A sound strategy can always be fine-tuned. Work programs can always be more cost-effective and productive. Managers can always find better ways of hiring and developing people. Supervisors can always manage people better. Leadership can always be more deeply ingrained in the institution. Total quality and constant learning are inseparable.

Constant Improvement and Employee Involvement Programs

Together these programs constitute a fifth building block. While constant improvement and employee involvement programs are often dealt with separately, the first cannot be done without the second. Constant improvement programs were developed in the United States and then, like Deming's approach to quality improvement, exported to Japan after World War II. Japanese businesses have a way of taking such programs very seriously, improving them, making them part of their culture, and finding endless ways of implementing them, while many U.S. companies find them difficult both to start and to maintain.

Toyota has won a preeminent place in the automotive industry by never being satisfied with its products. In his book *40 Years, 20 Million Ideas,* Yuzo Yasuda (1991) illustrates how Toyota's Creative Idea Suggestion System, a key way the firm involves its workers in continually improving the business, has contributed to the company's long-term success. The system generated over twenty million ideas in a forty-year period, and an astonishing 70 percent of these ideas were implemented. Toyota's program focuses on eliminating waste; solving problems such as machine stoppage; improving work design, including administrative and managerial work; and developing inventive manufacturing processes and tools.

Toyota not only learns but also disseminates its learning both inside and outside the company. Bumper Works, a small Illinois business and a Toyota supplier, is a case in point (see White, 1991). Sahid Kahn, founder and owner of the company, knew that Toyota could teach his firm little about engineering low-cost bumpers. But he soon learned that Toyota had a great deal to teach his company about how to run a bumper factory. The Japanese giant sent a team of manufacturing experts to conduct a crash course in the Toyota Production System. The result? Productivity jumped 60 percent within a year and the number of defects dropped by 80 percent. Such learning is not painless. Everyone at Bumper Works had to go through a gut-wrenching transformation process. Much of the plant and the work programs used in it were redesigned. The learning curve was steep for the small company, but in the end Toyota got the lower prices it expected and learned how it could effectively teach and train other suppliers, while the Bumper Works owner is applying his newly won learning to building a second factory.

Who should be on the constant improvement learning curve in any given company or institution? Everyone. Or at least that is the ideal. Current employee involvement programs may or may not be a fad, but the ideal is to have a critical mass of workers contributing their ideas on how to do things better. In Japan, the constant improvement process is called *kaizen*. Sometimes this process is called *constant incremental improvement* because many of the improvements suggested are small. But continuous small improvements can add up to explosive success. This is not to question the value of more dramatic "breakthrough" thinking and change. Some companies have prospered because of breakthroughs. Consider the enormously successful laser printer unit of Hewlett-Packard. The product itself, a laser printer for the office market priced under $4,000, was the fruit of breakthrough thinking. In 1983, when the product was first being developed, laser printers cost about $100,000 and were used with mainframes. Developing the printer at a Boise, Idaho, site far from the firm's California headquarters was critical to the breakthrough; the home office culture could have done the project in. Creating a printer that worked with competitors' personal computers was a breakthrough. Distributing the printer through retailers such as ComputerLand and Businessland was also a breakthrough. Restricting distribution to HP's direct sales force would have limited sales.

Constant improvement programs thrive in companies in which employees are empowered to think, learn, and act in ways that both enhance the business and improve quality of work life. Leaders, as we have seen earlier, both get people on board innovative projects and also do whatever is necessary to see to it that people's creative juices continue to flow. Good ideas will continue to well up from the shop floor, of course, to the degree that these ideas are rewarded. This does not automatically mean monetary rewards. The satisfaction of seeing one's good idea implemented is a reward in itself for many. In one sense, it is the highest reward. Recognition of good ideas is another reward. In 1871, Denny of Dumbarton, a Scottish shipbuilder, implemented one of the first suggestion systems in Britain, including cash awards (Denny & Bros., 1932):

> Any employee (exclusive of head foremen, officials of the Award Committee, and heads of departments) may claim an award from the committee on the following grounds:
>
> a) That he has invented or introduced a new machine or hand tool into the works.
> b) That he has improved any existing machine or hand tool.
> c) That he has applied any existing machine or hand tool to a new class of work.
> d) That he has discovered or introduced any new method of carrying on or arranging work.
> e) That he has invented or introduced any appliance for the prevention of accidents.
> f) That he has suggested some means by which waste of material may be avoided.
> g) Or, generally, that he has made any change by which work is rendered either superior in quality or more economical in cost.

Cash was awarded for each idea accepted by the committee, and a premium was awarded for every fifth idea accepted. Except for modifications in the sexist language to meet current social realities, the program as outlined could add value to many

companies today. The economics of well-run improvement programs are very good. Over a ten-year period, Canon invested
about \$2.2 million, mostly in prize money, but the return was
more than \$10 million. "Well run" is the operative description.
Many companies invest heavily in employee involvement programs, execute these poorly, and end up adding cost rather than
value.

Benchmarking

Benchmarking is a process of learning from other companies and
institutions that do things well. The term was first used to
describe a strategy initiated by Xerox in 1979 to reverse the
decline it suffered against tough Japanese competition throughout the 1970s. Xerox compared its manufacturing methods to
those of its Japanese affiliate, Fuji/Xerox, and of other highly
efficient Japanese competitors and then set up tight new systems to meet — and then exceed — those high standards.

    General Electric has also used benchmarking as a learn-
ing tool. Early on, the firm identified over twenty companies
that had achieved faster productivity growth than GE and had
sustained this growth for at least ten years. Since, for GE, benchmarking meant meeting with representatives of these companies and learning from them, GE managers eliminated direct
competitors from the list of possible partners. They also eliminated companies that might lack credibility in the eyes of GE
managers. They sent people out to learn the best practices of
their benchmarking partners, including Chaparral Steel, Ford,
Xerox, and Hewlett-Packard, and received return visits from
them. The company learned a great deal about interunit teamwork to speed products through the system, outhustling competitors in introducing new products, managing inventory so
that less capital is tied up, and treating suppliers as partners.
This partnership approach could be called "interactive" benchmarking.

    There is also "noninteractive" benchmarking. The nonin-
teractive benchmarking company uses the standards of any company, including direct competitors, that has achieved excellence

in any area relevant to its business. Good learners learn from others. They seek out best practice, adapt it to their own institutions, and then improve on what they have learned. Once Montgomery Ward had focused on value-focused specialty retailing as the core of its strategy, the company identified what it called a "stake in the ground" in each specialty area, that is, a successful specialty company serving customers and markets similar to its own. In other words, the company focused on exemplars in each specialty area. The company in no way wanted to be a slavish imitator, but it was willing to learn effective retailing and specialty store practices wherever they might be found. Retailers routinely shop their competitors' stores learning whatever they can to stay on the leading edge.

Learning from Change

Change of one type or another, a daily event in companies and institutions, is also a valuable source of learning. Chew, Leonard-Barton, and Bohn (1991), noticing the universal applicability of Murphy's Law, stressed organizational learning as a way to escape this law. Although they focus on the introduction of new technology, their recommendations apply to many different kinds of change. Their model turns the implementation of any project or program into a learning experience — one that can be immediately applied to the project at hand and used to make future projects easier to implement. They suggest four principles: (1) regard change projects as a form of R&D, (2) learn through simulations, (3) learn through pilot projects and prototypes, and (4) learn from obstacles to change.

1.   Regard Change Projects as a Form of R&D. The positioning and implementation of change is an R&D or learning effort in its own right. Therefore, companies should

   •   Learn from those who are to be affected by the change, for instance, those who will be using a new technology or those who have to make a new structure work. They will help you see obstacles you are overlooking. Also learn what kind of support will be needed by those affected by the change.

• Search out the weak links in change implementation. As one retailer moved to a new strategy, it needed general merchandising managers who could think strategically and who were capable of imparting a sense of strategy to store managers. Few such people were available.

• Enlarge the definition of the change project to include whatever linkages must be activated to deliver the change. A new information system in a hospital may mean that departments such as admissions and nursing will have to relate differently to each other. In this case change is not just about a new information system but about turf disputes.

• Experiment with new organizational forms as well as technical processes in order to support and sustain the change. For instance, self-managed teams might implement a new manufacturing technology better than standard supervisor-led teams.

This kind of "on-line" learning makes the implementation of current projects go more smoothly and builds up a storehouse of wisdom that can be applied to future projects.

2.   Learn Through Simulations. Construct models of the change effort. Do game-based or computer-based "dry runs" before the actual implementation of the change project. Simulations should have been used in many highway construction projects. Once a road is built, traffic saturation routinely takes place before forecast. In Britain, a freeway circling London hit capacity some ten years before forecast. The planners did not realize that the road would serve as a magnet for cars. Royal Dutch/Shell has been able to retain its preeminent position in its industry partly by having its managers learn through simulations. In one simulation, managers were forced to consider what would need to be done were oil ever to drop to fifteen dollars per barrel. The price at the time of the simulation was in the high twenties, with no drop in sight. However, not long after the simulation, OPEC collapsed and oil fell below fifteen dollars per barrel. Royal Dutch/Shell was better prepared than most. As mentioned earlier, however, all was not sweetness and light at Shell. Some managers complained that the planning group went overboard in the use of simulations and tied up too much staff time.

3.   Learn Through Pilot Projects and Prototypes. Implement changes in small, controlled projects. Learn from these and then do a major rollout. A child-abuse hot line was rolled out on national television in Britain. The telephone lines were overwhelmed with calls. Many children could not get through for days or even weeks. The well-intentioned sponsors could have quietly rolled out a pilot project in one part of the country to see what the response might be.

A prototype is a kind of pilot project. Michael Schrage (1991), who writes the innovation column for the *Los Angeles Times,* has called prototypes "building blocks for entrepreneurs." As such, they are tools for learning. Schrage does not necessarily refer to the slick and expensive prototypes that we read about and see in for instance, automotive magazines, the so-called concept cars. Rather he suggests converting ideas for new products into crude mock-ups and working models. These become a vehicle of learning and drive the innovation process. A California industrial design firm often generates as many as forty prototypes in designing a new product.

Prototyping need not be limited, of course, to products. A prototype of a new organizational structure can be designed on paper and used to elicit feedback from those who will have to make it work. A miniversion of the structure might even be set up in one of the company's smaller units. A rough chapter of a proposed book is a prototype that can be given to selected readers in order to get feedback.

Finally, as Schrage notes, crude prototypes — whether products, organizational structures, or book chapters — have their limitations. One limitation is illustrated by the saying, "Never show fools unfinished work."

4.   Learn from Obstacles to Change. This means two things. First, it means learn from others who have experienced difficulties implementing similar change efforts. One chemical company learned from a retailer that a good strategy has to be continually sold all around the place until a critical mass of implementers is obsessed with it. Second, it means learning from obstacles as they arise. Obstacles to change, however annoying, can be hidden treasures. Learning questions are, What do we have to do to make the new programs work? What do we have to change? What makes the implementation of change hard? Planning should provide a structure both for identifying problems and for managing them.

These, then, are some of the building blocks managers can use to create a learning organization culture. There is no single right way to do this. What do we need? What do we want? What is possible?

The Stages of a Learning Organization

Hall and Pedler (1989) describe a learning company as "an organization which facilitates the learning of all its members and continuously transforms itself in order to achieve its strategic aims." They outline three stages—efficiency, effectiveness, and transformation—through which a learning company can move on the way to meeting the challenges of the twenty-first century.

Level One: Efficiency

The focus of the first level is internal, and the goal is to become measurably more efficient. Included here are such things as improving productivity, however measured, cutting costs, improving internal systems such as the information management system and the incentive-reward system, developing better planning processes and control mechanisms, and improving communications. While these are essential, they are not the things that will keep the company ahead of the competition. To a degree, the mentality in Level One is survival. The company stops doing the wrong things.

Level Two: Effectiveness

The focus of Level Two is external, and the goal is to become measurably more effective. Included here are such things as creating competitive advantage, improving customer service, enhancing quality, and changing the product mix to fit the market and customers' needs and wants more effectively. The focus is on the business rather than the organization. While these activities will help the company "keep up with the Joneses" as it were, they will not necessarily place the firm in a leadership position. The Level Two mentality goes beyond survival, but it does not focus on industry leadership or preeminence.

Level Three: Transformation

The Level Three focus is both internal and external — on the organization and on business in an integrated way. The goal is transformation, becoming a "different business" and "doing business differently." It involves not just taking advantage of new opportunities but also creating new opportunities. For instance, it moves beyond the search for markets to the creation of new markets.

Competencies Needed in a Learning Organization

Many different competencies can go into any given institution's approach to business-enhancing learning. A few are reviewed here: anticipatory learning, double-loop learning, learning through debate, risk taking, learning from "noxiants," and learning from mistakes. These are reviewed below from the viewpoint of what they can contribute to organizational learning. These competencies are interrelated.

Anticipatory Learning: A Culture of Vigilance

Too many companies are taken by surprise by unexpected events. While it is true that many events are unexpected — merely consider the dramatic drop in oil prices a few years ago and the cataclysmic changes in Eastern Europe and what used to be the Soviet Union — it is also true that many so-called unexpected events are really events that could have been anticipated, at least in some fashion, but were not. Too few companies have a "culture of vigilance," an instinctive drive to continually scan both the internal and the external environment for threats and opportunities. Effective companies and institutions always have their antennas up. Anticipation, the capacity to foresee and prepare for new situations, is an extremely important component of the learning process. Increasing value-added options, which is the heart of learning, includes creating desirable futures for the institution, but this cannot be done without some degree of anticipation.

Consider the kind of learning currently needed by advertising agencies, since many of them are working under a cloud these days. Revenues for both advertising agencies and the media in which the ads are placed have slumped. This is partly due to the recession, but it might also point to a change in fundamentals. One wonders whether a bright agency, instead of counting on the glories of the past, might have identified the trends early on and adapted to them. There are several critical trends (see "What Happened," 1991). First of all, consumers, saturated with the bombardment of ads from every side, are tuning out. The average adult, bombarded with some three thousand marketing messages per day, has become immune or even cynical. In some cases, brand loyalty is eroding. Not every consumer believes that a brand name ensures quality. Second, companies are targeting customers through direct mail. For instance, Chrysler mailed a videotape dealing with the changes in its 1991 minivan to some 400,000 minivan owners. Technology is available to deliver messages to a market of one: "We have just the product for you, Tom Brown!" Market niche targeting has grown enormously. Third, money that used to go into advertising is now going into promotions to boost sagging revenues: coupons, contests, sweepstakes galore.

Although it is true that companies tend to pare advertising budgets as revenues sag, industry analysts suggest that fundamental changes are brewing. Those in charge of advertising strategies are looking at a whole range of marketing options: less advertising and more public relations, event sponsoring, promotions, telemarketing, direct mail marketing, and others. Alert companies continually ask themselves, What are the best ways for us to reach customers?

None of this, of course, means that advertising as we know it is going to go away. Advertising does work, even though it is often not clear just how. Nor are brands, nurtured by advertising, about to disappear. But things are changing in significant ways. Companies in a learning mode with competence in anticipatory learning will be in the lead in these changes.

Anticipatory learning requires the skill to separate environmental signals and messages from environmental noise. Companies good at anticipatory learning have models and maps that enable them to spot threats, opportunities, and trends. These include strategies that are continually updated, a system for scanning the competitive environment, and a system for scanning the internal environment. Anticipatory learning, then, is not just an exercise in imagination. While imagination is important, hard data are just as important. Only when anticipatory learning pervades an institution can the institution be said to have a "culture of vigilance." Assess, anticipate, innovate, add value. The Pan Ams and TWAs of this world did not learn that lesson.

Double-Loop Learning: Learning to Learn

Innovative companies and institutions are learning systems. This demands open inquiry and self-criticism, the basis for double-loop learning (Argyris, 1990). In double-loop learning, not only is feedback used to correct errors, but learner-participants step outside the system to question the very assumptions on which it operates. It does little good to keep improving a marketing strategy when the strategy itself has outlived its usefulness. Learning is not enough. Companies and institutions that want to continually increase their productivity must move on to learning how to learn; as Argyris (1990, p. 91) says, "The whole process of learning to learn hinges on the ability to remain open to changes occurring in the environment and to challenge operating assumptions in a most fundamental way." Double-loop learning depends on openness to change, an understanding of the inevitability of uncertainty and error, the ability to explore different viewpoints, opening even cherished hypotheses and assumptions to challenge and possible disconfirmation, and commitment to inquiry-driven action. Until recently, many of the

oil giants did not question the assumptions from which they oper-
ated. Then, all of a sudden, all of them were driven into a cost-
cutting mode. The best will now question their approach to
learning.

Learning Through Debate: Promoting Productive Conflict

As many theoreticians and practitioners have demonstrated,
conflict, when well managed, is an important stimulus for learning. Companies on the leading edge not only learn through
conflict that arises naturally but also promote conflict, contention, and debate because of their contribution to learning.

According to Richard Pascale (1990), structure in large
organizations is a split-and-fit proposition. First, these organizations split into divisions and teams to get the work done.
Through decentralization, units take onwership of certain problems and issues more actively and creatively. This serves as an
antidote to the vexing problem stated succinctly in the saying,
"What belongs to everyone belongs to no one." Second, the work
that is divided up must be brought back together again in order
to deliver the company's products and services to customers,
so interunit teamwork or "fit" is essential. Split-and-fit leads
naturally to tension. A degree of restless tension in an organization stimulates learning and keeps the firm from complacency.

According to Pascale, Hewlett-Packard's smoothing over
conflicts between divisions has inhibited the firm's speed to market, while Honda is one of the companies that uses conflict as
a vehicle for learning. Honda aims at a kind of restlessness and
uneasiness that heightens productivity. Of course, if tension is
too high and conflict turns into internecine war, then learning
will be interrupted and innovation and productivity will suffer.
Tension at Citicorp has at times been so high as to promote
learning-limiting insecurity. According to Pascale, there is a
"zone of constructive tension" that optimizes learning. Of course,
this zone will differ from institution to institution. Finally, a
strong sense of mission, a shared vision, and shared values—
provided that these do not constitute a straightjacket—create
a climate in which conflict can become a stimulus for learning.

Learning Through Risk Taking

Organizations and institutions that get ahead often take risks, at least reasonable risks. There are many different degrees of risk taking. Choosing different colored pencils is a far cry from betting the company on a new strategy. One international airline wanted to upgrade its business-class operations because of the fierceness of the competition. However, this meant spending a great deal of money doing research to get the markets right, refurbishing its planes, retraining some of its flight attendants to ensure top-flight service, and mounting an expensive advertising campaign. The company realized that in a highly competitive market there were risks in targeting business travelers and risks in not doing so. In the end, the company believed that it was more risky to sit and wait.

Bill Wriston (1986), the former CEO of Citicorp, took the business press to task for admonishing companies that adopt "risky strategies." He said that there is no accomplishment without risk and that if managers do not take risks, they should be thrown out of their offices. Citicorp took great risks and reaped the benefits of success. But then the banking world shifted and risky strategies that proved profitable in the short run were either managed poorly or turned sour. In sum, there is a middle ground between strategies that are reasonably risky and those that are merely foolhardy.

Learning from "Noxiants"

While implementing the slogan "set goals and go for it" is often quite stimulating and productive, it can also be limiting. This approach often fails because it naively avoids shadow side realities that prevent goals from being accomplished. Paradoxically, learning how to identify and avoid what Morgan (1986) calls *noxiants,* those things that stand in the way of accomplishing goals, can increase a company's degree of freedom to act. Once a broad strategy is formulated, managers should take time to brainstorm answers to the question What factors, both out there and in here, can do this strategy in? This, far from being an exercise in futility, launches a process of inquiry that uncovers strategic possibilities that mere goal setting would have ignored. Within constraints lie possibilities.

While companies can learn from noxiants as they arise, they can also take a preventive approach. Capitalizing on what others have learned from managing noxiants is a key step in the learning process. One of the learning rules devised by Chew, Leonard-Barton, and Bohn (1991) for installing new technology is to seek out others with experience and ask about the noxiants: "Ask 'What made it hard?' Not 'How well did it work?'" (p. 9). The question, How well does the technology work? while important, bypasses a range of precious learnings. If the technology does not work well, there is no use going any further. Questions of greater importance are, What were the stumbling blocks? How can they be avoided? What were the hardest things to do? What did you do to make the technology work? What did you have to change?

Learning from Mistakes

Since risk taking means that people will on occasion make mistakes, the relationship between making mistakes and learning needs to be reviewed. In this regard, one case is often cited. A senior manager makes a mistake that costs the company $1 million. He is called to a meeting of the top management team. Of course, he goes in fear and trepidation of being fired. In fact, in the meeting he says something to the effect, "So I assume that you are going to fire me." The CEO looks at him and says, "Fire you! Of course not. We've just spent $1 million on your education. You have to stay here so we can get a return on our investment."

Reactions to mistakes are hardly always this benign (or benighted, depending on your point of view). An institution's real (versus merely espoused) policy concerning mistake making has much to do with the climate of learning. While practically every institution admits that making mistakes and learning from them is and should be part of institutional life, not nearly as many turn policy into practice. Mistakes, even those from which there is both individual and institutional learning, are subtly punished. Career moves, if not blocked, are put on hold; bonuses are withheld. Displeasure lurks behind the "let's all of us learn from this" language. Part of the problem here is balance. While it is silly to extol learning from mistakes to the point where silly risks are taken and viability of the institution itself is jeopardized, it is just as silly to have a covert "no mistakes here" policy. A "we succeed or we learn" policy has its merits, but it also has its limits. There are no formulas that apply to every company and institution. Where is the balance point on the continuum between a "no mistakes here" policy and an "all mistakes are routinely forgiven" one?

One of the problems in answering this question is that few companies take the time to analyze the productivity derived from the learning associated with mistake making. Rather the tendency is to forgive the occasional benign mistake and hope that it does not happen again, or at least not frequently. To determine the productivity-related learning gained from mistake making, supervisors would have to take a much more active role. They would have to sit down with the person who has made the mistake and, through analysis, make sure that learning is derived and that the probability of further mistake making, at least in the same area of endeavor, is lessened or eliminated. In this process both supervisor and subordinate could estimate the value of the learning. In one company, an analysis of a glaring mistake by one manager led to the discovery that many managers were making the same mistake but of a lesser magnitude. In this case the return on the effort made to analyze the mistake was enormous.

When these abilities are consistently turned into patterns of action (for instance, when a company consistently learns from its mistakes), then there is a culture of learning. Many companies and institutions learn, but the company with a learning organization culture does so consistently and in a wide variety of ways.

The Shadow Side of a Learning Organization

It is easy to see that there are many pitfalls on the road to becoming a learning organization and then staying on the learning

track. The shadow side is everywhere. But, once more, forewarned is forearmed.

The Fad Pitfall

The first, and perhaps obvious, pitfall is "fadism." Owners and
managers are often looking for the magic that will turn the place
around. Many business-enhancing movements, even excellent
ones such as total quality management and customer service,
have a fad dimension to them. This is to be expected. I am sure
that right now many managers cringe as they notice the number of articles being generated about the learning organization,
saying to themselves, "Oh-oh, here comes the next barrage from
the corner office." However, many managers could also say to
themselves, "This is a good idea even though there is a lot of
hoopla associated with it right now." The task is to take the best
of what is offered even in a "fad" and incorporate it into the system; it must get into the fabric of the company. The concept
of the learning organization is popular right now, at least in
the literature. In a couple of years perhaps no one will use the
term, but effective companies will still be deeply invested in
learning. A commitment to the kind of learning that leads to
continual improvement is common sense.

The Name Pitfall

The term *learning organization* might sound too intellectual, aca-
demic, or abstract for some managers. Let it be called whatever
makes sense for the particular institution. Companies with TQM
programs need not change the name or add another program.
The best ideas from the "learning organization" literature can
be folded into the TQM process. In the end, what is important
is the culture, not the name. Some companies and institutions
have developed a culture of learning without naming it anything.

The Culture-Change Pitfall

For many companies and institutions, becoming a learning organization is a substantial culture change that can be achieved

only over time. While substantive changes in the culture itself are often slow, patterns of behavior can be changed in a shorter period of time. For instance, a company does not need years to set up processes to uncover conflicts that are routinely swept under the rug and to initiate debate around the issues uncovered. It does not take years to see to it that managers participate in basic communication and conflict management skills. While all of this will not immediately change conflict-avoiding attitudes, the company can begin to act its way into new modes of thinking. As managers discover that their careers are not terminated just because they disagree with mainstream ideas, and as the company discovers that debate begets ideas that actually make it more productive, its "personality," that is, its culture, can begin to evolve.

The Learning Disabilities Pitfall

Senge has noted that organizations, like individuals, have their "learning disabilities." Overcoming or at least managing these is essential if a culture of learning is to emerge. He has identified a range of these disabilities.

Job Description Fixation. This is the "I am my position" disability. This narrow focus on job description or role can lock a person into a narrow range of thinking and acting and restrict learning. "I am a chemical engineer" should read "I am an agent of this company's strategy, principally but not solely in the area of chemical engineering." Such a statement opens the doors to learning. Job or role flexibility can help get people out of the "I am my job" mentality. Sometimes unions oppose greater job flexibility — and therefore the learning that comes with it — not because they are against job flexibility in itself but because they fear that greater job flexibility will lead to a loss of jobs. In many cases where this conflict between management and unions over job flexibility has been overcome, learning and productivity have surged even without a loss of jobs.

Blaming Others. This is the "the enemy is out there" disability. Effective managers look for creative solutions; drone managers look for someone to blame. Problems and failures usually have multiple causes. Seeking these causes out, including failures due to one's own ineptitude, in order to learn from them is an upbeat activity. If managers say, "We have a poor workforce," then it is fair to ask, "What do you do to merit a poor workforce?"

The Tyranny of Events. Managers preoccupied with events such as last month's or last week's sales figures, the budget cuts, the new structure, turnover figures, product introductions, recalls of defective products, and the like do not see and learn from the patterns embedded in or lurking behind these events. In the heat of battle critical incidents and trends are ignored. The directors of a group of YMCA facilities in the Midwest were thunderstruck when they saw the figures on declining memberships and were faced with the issue of survival. For the first time, they had to ask, "What's going on here?" They had been too preoccupied with the daily, weekly, and monthly operational events of their facilities.

Becoming More Ignorant Through Experience. The common belief that we automatically learn through experience is often just a delusion. No doubt experience can be a powerful and harsh teacher, but too often managers do not really experience the effects of their decisions. In one large institution, training was arbitrarily dropped because of the need to cut costs. The director who made the decision saw costs go down, but he did not see the losses in productivity that came from ineptitude and demoralization. Through experience some managers merely learn how to rationalize their behavior more effectively.

The Institution-Limiting Team. While Senge sees the team as the principal learning unit within a company or institution, this hardly means that all teams are bastions of learning. Many teams stand in the way of organization learning by protecting their turf, making weak decisions through compromise, and avoiding conflict. Lowest common denominator teams neither learn nor stimulate learning. History has shown that management teams afflicted with "group think" not only do not learn but also make decisions that have devastating consequences.

The "Defensive Routines" Pitfall

According to Argyris's (1977, 1986, 1990, 1991) notion of "defensive routines," a major pitfall on the road to becoming a learning organization is that many managers do not know how to learn. We have identified "learning how to learn" as an important institutional skill above. However, those who should be best at learning — professionals who occupy key leadership positions — are often the poorest learners.

Managers often use their intelligence to sabotage learning. They confuse problem solving with learning. While one can certainly learn through problem solving, problem solving and learning are not the same thing. The manager who looks inward and asks, "How do I contribute to this institution's problems" is stepping outside the problem-solving loop and is on the threshold of double-loop learning, that is, learning how to learn. But this seems to happen infrequently with the best and the brightest. When bright managers are asked to criticize a project constructively, they practically never cite their own limitations. They are well aware of the limitations of others, however. This defensiveness does not stem from these managers' professional attitudes about change or continuous improvement. Indeed, they do not even know that they are being defensive. And these are very bright people.

According to Argyris, the working model these managers use to defend themselves has four clandestine values: to stay in unilateral control, to maximize "winning" and minimize "losing," to suppress negative feelings, and to be as "rational" as possible. By pursuing these values, they avoid embarrassment, threat, feelings of vulnerability, feelings of incompetence, and the fear of the fear of failure. But they also avoid learning and a whole host of opportunities to add value. We all know managers like this; we see them in the mirror daily.

What can be done about this game? Questioning the commitment of these managers to learning, directly confronting their defensiveness, and changing structures in order to encourage learning behavior do not work. The key to change is awareness. Argyris has suggested that one major step is to have senior managers examine their own behavior and identify their own defensive routines. If senior managers do not examine their defensiveness, they will not support efforts on the part of middle managers to examine their own.

The royal route to change, according to Argyris, is to tie the entire change process to the business, that is, to get the principals involved in an analysis of real business-focused cases. He provides a methodology to help senior managers get at their own defensive routines and to share their findings with the members of their teams. The business-focused case study legitimizes a discussion of defensive routines as such and, since the senior managers are openly talking about and soliciting feedback on their own defensiveness, "permission" is given to everyone to discuss his or her own defensiveness. A safe atmosphere for doing so is provided. This does not mean that these discussions are without pain. But, as Argyris has noted, through this process managers and management teams "are learning about their own group dynamics. . . . The insights they gain will allow them to act more effectively in the future. . . . They are not just solving problems but developing a far deeper and more textured understanding of their role as members of the organization. They are laying the groundwork for continuous improvement that is truly continuous. They are learning how to learn" (1991, p. 109).

The Control Pitfall

While too little control can do in the business, too much control can drive out learning. Unfortunately, many companies and institutions in our society, like many individuals, are in controlling rather than learning modes even though the rate at which a company or institution learns may be the only source of sustainable competitive advantage. While "friendly" controls are essential, overcontrol blocks learning. All of us are familiar with individual learning, but institutional learning differs from individual learning in that it takes place through shared insights, knowledge, and models among the workforce. Defective internal links, mainly managers who are in a controlling rather than learning mode, can block or slow institutional learning.

NINE

The Way Forward:
Taking Action
and Adding Value

Models A, B, and C provide the infrastructure for business, managerial, and leadership effectiveness. Read the business literature. Visit companies that are currently on the cutting edge. Talk to the best people in your own company or department. Explore your own imagination. You will find dozens of good ideas for improving your business. You can prevent these innovations from becoming mere fads by embedding them in the infrastructure of your company or institution. The president of a small company located in Indiana once said, "We know who we are, what we are about, the world in which we do business, and what we need to do both to stay afloat and to get better. And we deal straightforwardly with the junk that gets in our way. What more do we need than that?" He was talking about the essentials, the infrastructure of his company, his models of management. Building infrastructure may not be glamorous work, but without it nothing else matters.

An Advanced Organizer: What Chapter Nine Is About

- *The Primacy of Model A.* While Models B and C are essential and, at first glance, seem more sexy than Model A, Model A has primacy because it deals with the basic needs of the company or institution.

- *Possible Steps Forward.* There are several things both individual managers and teams can do to move forward: simply act on insights gleaned, conduct an audit to "take the pulse" of the business, take an audit of shared models already in place in order to strengthen and add to them, pursue a benchmarking approach, start with one of the models or with a part that makes immediate sense for the business, develop in-house versions of any of these models, or set up a management development program based on Models A, B, and C.
- *Crossing Borders: Adding Value Abroad.* Models A, B, and C can be adapted to a variety of cultural contexts.
- *Targets for the Shared Models Approach.* Although the focus in this book has been on companies and institutions, there are ways in which both business schools and consulting firms could benefit from this approach.

Presenting the case for shared models of managing is the easy part. Implementation, as usual, is the hard part. While some companies have developed a reasonably comprehensive approach to managing that is shared—for example, TQM is used by some, marketing by others—and other companies have bits and pieces of shared models, very few have taken the kind of comprehensive approach outlined in this book. This presents not just problems but also opportunities and challenges.

The Primacy of Model A

When I briefly outline Models A, B, and C to seminar audiences and then say, "Well, we really have time for only one of the three, so which one do you want?" the choices are predictable. The first choice is Model C. The second is Model B. Model A comes third. This order is both understandable and a cause for concern.

The choice of Model C is understandable because, if a great deal of time and energy are spent managing the arationality of the organization, it makes sense to learn a framework and develop tools for managing the shadow side. My fear, however, is that, in choosing Model C, people may be looking for two things: initiation into the mysteries of the organization and acquisition of the magic needed to make the enterprise work. Model C helps in the consciousness-raising process and puts some order into the shadow side. In this sense, it demystifies the organization. One manager, halfway through a course on Model C, said, "Now that I've lost my organizational innocence, what do I do to manage these shadow side realities?" There is no magic but only understanding, skills, and managerial courage. Effective managers in their search for wisdom learn the ways in which Model C categories permeate all the activities of the institution, come to understand and pay attention to the shadow side, acquire skills and tools for dealing with such shadow side realities as organizational politics and culture, and develop the courage to use these skills in the pursuit of both productivity and quality of work life.

The preference for Model B, instituting and managing change, over Model A is also understandable. People, including myself, like to see themselves as agents of business-enhancing change. Furthermore, there are so many problems to be managed and so many opportunities to be developed that the need for a shared model of making institution-enhancing change happen is a top priority. The drawback is this: since a model of making change happen is a process model, it is only as good as the content of that process. To answer such critical questions as What is going on? What should we change? What are our preferred-scenario possibilities? Which of these makes most sense for us? expertise in content, that is, the relevant master tasks and subtasks of Model A, is essential.

Therefore, while all three models are essential managerial tools, Model A still has primacy. It deals with the most important question of all: What does this company need to be effective and how do our managers meet these needs? Because it is a model of how to make things work, the other models are subordinate to it. As already noted, Model A provides templates for both the assessment and the preferred scenario stages of Model B. Model C realities, as important as they are, do not exist in a vacuum but rather permeate all the master tasks of Model A and the stages of Model B. Model C deals with style, or the ways in which members at all levels of an institution pursue their work. Without Model A, Model C and Model B are devoid of substantial content.

Competent managers move seamlessly within and among these three models. For them these models and methods are channels of common sense. If stopped in midcourse, they would be able to tell you what mix of models and methods they were using at the moment, but as they grow more proficient, they become less interested in naming what they are doing than in getting it done. Most managers already do many of the things suggested by these three models. One manager introduced to Model B responded, "I think I do a lot of these things already. But now I know what I am doing and have a process map to guide me. I also realize that my change efforts were not as effective and efficient as they might have been because there were steps that I was overlooking. For instance, I tend to move from diagnosis to action strategies right away. Working on the preferred scenario first will in the long run save me time and give the company a better product." Comprehensive shared models of management help managers organize what they are already doing well and begin to do other things that will add even more value to their work.

Possible Steps Forward

This book presents an ideal, but it is a pragmatic ideal. The package of models presented is not an all-or-nothing proposition. The shared models thesis of this book is meant to stimulate debate in companies and institutions about management, not to provide instant solutions. Still, the messages are meant to guide behavior, and some suggestions for moving forward are outlined in this chapter. While individual managers will find some of them useful, the power of these suggestions lies in their being pursued by groups of managers within a company. What is important is not just the models or tailored versions of them, but their being shared. Ways toward achieving such a team approach include simple consciousness-raising and individual action, "taking the pulse" of the business, conducting an audit and critique of shared models already in place, benchmarking, and adopting in-house versions of Models A, B, and C and using them for management development programs.

Simple Consciousness-Raising

At minimum, managers should glean an idea here or there in the shared models approach that strikes them as useful. For instance, one manager was interested in the possibilities of job flexibility and experimented with cross-training in his unit. The unit benefited from increased productivity, and the workers, for the most part, enjoyed the variety. One employee discovered a knack for computers. He revised the work practices in his area and then automated many of them, thus making a major contribution. A manager in another company, on reading an earlier version of Model A, was struck by General Electric's "workout" approach to work redesign and simplification. She prepared a version of the model and estimated that her department would save about fifty thousand dollars per year. She shared her "experiment" with her boss and a workout process was designed for the entire company. While her individual effort was quite successful, the real payoff came when the workout process became a shared model of managing.

"Taking the Pulse" of the Business

Model A can be used to "take the pulse" of a company or any of its units. There are various approaches to such an audit. First, I have used interviews to help many manager groups conduct audits. I ask them, individually, open-ended questions based on the master tasks of Model A: How important is strategy around here? How does it get formulated? What happens once it gets formulated? and similar questions in other master task areas. I then use Model A categories to summarize my findings and feed them back to the group. While I look for themes, I try to avoid interpretations of what they say.

Once they get the feedback, which includes some of their own individual statements to make sure they realize that this is their data, not mine, I teach them the basics of Model B. They use Model B to prioritize the problems, opportunities, and challenges that have been uncovered and to search for solutions in terms of preferred scenarios and action strategies. In the feedback report I also share the culture themes that permeate their responses. To one manager I said, "You have a very substantial strategy," then asked, "Are you guys going to deliver the goods?" He looked at me, paused, and then said, "Not the way we do things here." We went on to explore dimensions of the culture that did not support the strategy.

In most cases, after several such interviews, certain clearcut culture themes emerge. The feedback report inevitably has some beneficial shock effect. Often this is the first time an entire range of critical issues gets into a public forum in an unvarnished way.

I have also used surveys based on Model A to help managers assess their areas of concern. These surveys are similar to the "360s" discussed earlier, but they focus on the performance of the company or unit itself rather than that of individual managers. In one company the survey results had a dramatic impact on the senior team. The survey report, dealing with the strategy master task, was presented in graphic form. It had three lines on it representing different respondents or groups of respondents. The first line represented the view of the president; the second, the composite views of his direct reports; the third, the composite views of fifty "key informants" further down in the organization. Across the strategy subtasks the lines moved in unison, that is, a rise or a dip in any given category such as vision or core competencies was reflected in each line. But the direct reports' line was some ten points below the president's, and the key informants' line was ten points below that of the direct reports. "What's going on here?" exclaimed the president. Over the next two days it became clear: many saw strategy as a meaningless "numbers" game, few believed they had any input into it, the strategy did not permeate all levels of the company, and it did not drive behavior. This revelation kicked off a revolution of sorts within the company, with work on the mission, vision, and values part of strategy starting almost immediately.

Some colleagues and I have used a simple audit tool, *Taking the Pulse* (Egan & McGourty, in press), to help managers, in a workshop format, do an initial "physical" on the company or unit. A computerized version of the audit allows team of managers to give themselves instant feedback in any Model A category and to explore the implications of the feedback. In one company the managers said, "None of us believes that we have the right strategy and true strategic leadership. Let's get down to business and determine what we want." Since this audit covers all six master tasks, just as a physical covers the main functions of the body, it prevents managers from prematurely focusing on one issue. In the example just mentioned, the managers finally said, "We've all been grousing about the structure, but if we believe that we don't have the right strategy, how could we possibly know whether we've got the right structure or not?" The audit process helps managers get a feel for the models and is thus a first step in determining what kind of shared models they need.

An Audit and Critique of Existing Shared Models

Another starting point is an audit of shared models of managing already in place. What management paradigms do we work from? If managers develop an understanding of the shared models of management that are already in place, they can strengthen those that serve the business, challenge those that do not really add value, and adopt others that will provide leverage. In one company, the consensus sounded like this: "The only two shared models of management we really have around here are the budget system and the performance appraisal system. Neither serves us very well because both are outmoded control systems. The former is too rigid. It is not based on the ever-changing needs of our business. And everyone hates the latter. Everyone sees the need for budgetary controls, but the appraisal system gives us control without benefits."

The managers in another company used the Model A framework to take a look at an off-the-shelf employee empowerment program they had purchased about a year earlier. Their findings went something like this: "While we were very enthusiastic about this process in the beginning, it has not worked well for us. First of all, the language it uses is not our language and we have failed to adapt it to our company. The training programs sound phony to most of our employees. Second, the program is a stand-alone process. It is not linked to our business. Third, we now believe that we could design a better program — one that will meet our needs and fit our culture — ourselves. We underestimated our own abilities."

The audit can also be a needs assessment, a determination of what kinds of shared models would benefit the company. The managers of the company cited in the previous paragraph went on to say, "Fourth, and most important, against a broader framework (Model A), this employee empowerment program is not our top priority. Our competitors are far ahead of us on quality. We thought that we could catch up by generating more enthusiasm through an empowerment program. Now that assumption seems simplistic and naive. We need to improve both our manufacturing processes and our products. And we need to do that right away."

An audit helped a distributor of industrial parts discover that a companywide approach to selling was one of its primary needs. Given limited resources, they put a team-building program on hold. An audit helped the partners in a counseling practice realize that their shared approach to counseling was one of their major strengths. But they also discovered that they were in desperate need of some shared financial models. They were running a business without business skills. They had no models to deal with the economics of such things as office space, professional development, and marketing.

A Benchmarking Approach

Here *benchmarking* means finding out what shared models of managing are being used by other companies, evaluating how well they are working, and determining which ones can be tailored to meet the needs of the company. For instance, managers of one oil company visited General Electric to review both business and human resource models. When they came back, they instituted a version of GE's approach to training and evaluating managers. Since they already had a number of human resource programs in the pipeline, they made sure the GE approach, which focused on both managers' productivity and their "people" style, complemented these human resource initiatives. The new director of management development at a large international development bank visited five companies reported to have the best management development programs in the country. When he came back, he and his team members sifted through the findings. They ended up using their own original framework for the program, but borrowed and adapted some individual modules from programs in these other companies. Models A, B, and C can be used to identify shared models of management being used in other companies, to locate them on a business, organizational, managerial, and leadership map, and to determine which ones would add value.

Direct Use of Models A, B, or C

Some companies adopt one or another model or just parts of them. Many companies I work with have been quick to adopt Model B, but slower to appreciate the benefits of some form of Model A. In some of these companies, the change process is routinely used for both problem solving and planning larger change projects. The language of Model B — "turning problems into opportunities," "preferred scenario," "bias for action," "little preplan actions," "inertia," "entropy," and the like — has entered day-to-day discourse. And some businesses use their own language. One group asks, "Where are you on the action curve?"

A partner in Britain uses the strategy part of Model A as one of the major bases for his consultation practice with senior managers. He has translated it from American into English and produced a variety of handouts that help managers use strategy as a tool instead of just as a concept. He talks about the rest of Model A — operations, structure, human resource management systems, management and supervisory systems, and leadership — all in terms of "strategic leadership." He is helping a bank train its loan officers in the strategic subtasks of Model A so that they can better determine the viability of the businesses to which they are making loans.

A British consulting group that specializes in TQM programs uses Model A to get at the "total" part of their programs. Model A is routinely shared with clients who are then asked what master task areas call for quality. The almost inevitable answer is, "Well, ideally, all of them." Then it is a question of where to start, and different companies take different routes to quality. Since total quality management processes call for a problem-solving or change model, this consulting group teaches the basic elements of Model B to their clients.

In a manufacturing concern, a plant manager, after a seminar in which Model B had been presented, used it to give structure to the Monday morning meetings with his direct reports. These meetings had often been disorganized and conflict-ridden. The Monday after the seminar he taught the basics of Model B. Then when each issue came up, employees discussed blind spots, the preferred scenario, and ways of bringing it on-line, made decisions, and collectively assigned both responsibilities and deadlines. One direct report told the plant manager that the meeting was the best he had ever attended. This Model B process is still in place. There is nothing magical about the models — or any model for that matter. Rather, a simple version of Model B served an immediate need and served it well.

Many companies have focused on the performance management system as discussed in Model A, realizing that theirs fell into the "cost center" rather than the "profit center" category. Most have discovered how difficult it is to get away from an appraisal/control mentality and move to a performance improvement focus. The culture does not change easily. Performance management in many companies is a good target, for the reasons mentioned in Chapter Five. It is, or should be, one of the most comprehensive of the submodels, because it focuses on strategy, empowerment, work program design, two-way communication, coaching/counseling, friendly controls, people development, and the incentive/reward system in a never-ending cycle. One company in Britain, after doing a Model A audit, dropped its performance management system for a year and used the money that would have been spent to administer it to design a system based on these profit center concepts. Interestingly enough, even though there was no performance management system, no one stopped working that year.

Some companies have taken a more wide-reaching approach to incorporating versions of the these three basic models — or similar models of their own making — into the fabric of the company, with varying degrees of success. One telecommunications company trained its internal consultants in Models A, B, and C. The members of this unit used these frameworks to help line managers cope with the needs of the business and the almost delirious rate of change that characterized that industry. This venture fell apart when massive cost-cutting measures eliminated this and a host of other programs.

One airline took the same approach. However, the training of the human resource professionals who were to become internal consultants was somewhat perfunctory. Moreover, the vice president of human resources failed to get the line vice presidents on board this scheme. Line managers wondered why the human resource managers were not getting on with their accustomed "personnel" duties.

Developing In-House Versions of Models A, B, and C

In 1992 Amoco Chemical Company promulgated its own shared models approach. In 1991 all the members of the management committee of the company had been trained in Baldrige National Quality Award criteria, not necessarily to apply for the award but as a means of self-assessment and improvement. But Jim Fligg, the president, thought that the Baldrige criteria did not cover such things as strategic planning and financial performance or environment, health, and safety concerns. So the company extracted the underlying management principles of the Baldrige criteria and complemented them with principles derived from the company's mission, vision, and values. The resulting vision-oriented management framework is outlined in Figure 9.1. It is evident that this is the company's Model A.

Figure 9.1. Amoco Chemical's Version of Model A.

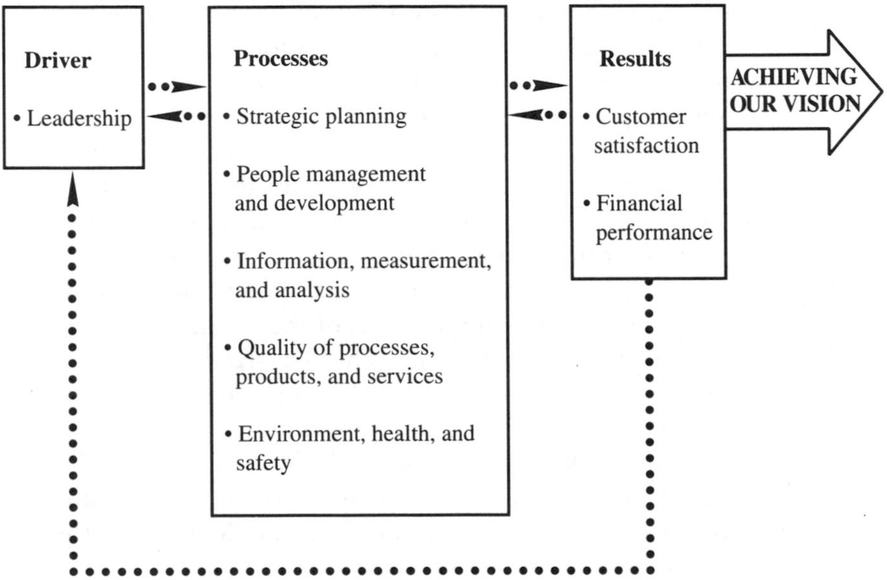

These principles were published in *Amoco Chemical Management Principles — A Framework for Competitive Leadership and Continuous Improvement,* a document detailing what each of the concepts in Figure 9.1 means. Fligg wanted this framework to be the principal shared model of managing within the company, and its principles were to be used by everyone — from first-line supervisor to the executive committee — in day-to-day management. The framework is integrative, pulling together the Baldridge criteria, the company's quality improvement process, and the company's mission-vision-values principles and linking all of these to the company's strategic plans for continual renewal. Indeed, many of the company's employees were grateful for this management framework, because it was not just one more program but a consolidation of all major management initiatives. The vision of Amoco Chemical is to be recognized as the industry exemplar by its customers, competitors, shareholders, employees, and the public, to grow and be profitable, to be truly global in scope, to develop innovative products and businesses, and to be known as a preferred employer and good corporate citizen.

Also in 1992, Montgomery Ward took a different approach, a structural one, to business and management effectiveness. As noted previously, the company had already developed and was well into implementing its specialty retailing strategy, "Focus on the Future." The company had also developed a customer service strategy, "Focus on the Customer," but, like many other companies, was disappointed in the implementation of that strategy.

Finally, Bernard Brennan, the chair and CEO, knowing how essential it was to get everyone on board to achieve these initiatives, began spelling out the company's people development strategy, "Focus on People." An executive vice presidency was established to promote all three initiatives. Cascading and implementing strategy, promoting customer service as an operational strategic driver, and leveraging the human assets of the company as an organizational strategic driver were considered so important and so interrelated that they were dramatized to the entire company by the establishment of a new structure and by naming a line manager as the vice president of strategy and organizational development. A new director of customer service, a person who was to assume the role of customer advocate, and a new head of people development joined the team. The job of the team was to help all managers, indeed, all associates, make the "leadership triangle" (illustrated in Figure 9.2) work.

The job of the director of development was to set up the development and training programs needed to empower associates to make the integrated strategy, customer service, and development process work. Another way of putting this is that the strategy, especially as cascaded down into every organizational unit, and the customer service focus specified the major needs of the business. Now, developing managers and associates to meet these needs was crucial. This also had to be done cost-effectively. Therefore, every manager was expected to be a developer of himself or herself and a developer of people.

Figure 9.2. Montgomery Ward's Strategic Leadership Triangle.

Using the Models as a Basis for a Management Development Program

Insofar as Models A, B, and C focus on the ever-changing needs of the business, by inference they suggest the kinds of supervisory, managerial, and leadership skills needed to meet these needs. I have worked with several institutions that have used these models or parts of them as the basis for management development programs, some of them quite extensive. The process, at least ideally, goes something like this. Model A is first used to take the pulse of the system. Once the needs of the company are identified, the next task is to determine how well equipped managers are to meet these needs. Once the gap is identified, managers' needs, based now on business needs, are translated into development and training programs. This differs quite substantially from the off-the-shelf approach.

Pieces of Models A, B, and C were used some years ago to put together for a large international development institution a three-week management development program spread out over a year. Week one was spent helping managers review both their personal and their managerial styles, including communication skills. This week included a "360"—feedback from boss, peers, direct reports, and self on managerial style and effectiveness. The second week focused on the managers' ability to supervise others and build teams. The third week focused on the manager as manager of business processes, including strategy and its implementation, instituting and managing change, and both challenging the current culture and developing the preferred one.

If I had to do this over again, I would probably reverse that order. I would start with the needs of the business — perhaps a miniaudit of the company or the unit that would include all six master tasks. Next, I would take a good look at the state of human resource management systems, how they might need to be changed, and how creative the manager might be in using them to supervise others. The "360s" could be used at this point together with some training in communication skills. Finally, I would help managers take a look at themselves, their needs, and their personal styles. These needs should be balanced with the demands of the business. Time management programs are helpful at this stage.

Surveys indicate that very few institutions provide this much training for their managers — nowhere near it. Therefore, on-the-job learning and developing are essential. Consider this case. A manager in one company said that one of her managers was "superb" at marketing but "devastating" with people. It was suggested that he be sent to "charm school" somewhere. I pointed out that one of the principles of Model A in the area of development was that training (school) was one of the more expensive approaches to development and therefore should be used to complement other forms of development. In this case the "devastating" manager's supervisor was overlooking the difference between "can't" and "won't." She was assuming that since this manager did not deal well with people that he could not, at least not without the help of a training program. I set up an experiment. I worked with the problematic manager and his direct reports. I found out how the direct reports saw him — as an unprofessional, unbusinesslike, and downright offensive supervisor. I fed these messages back to the manager.

I then sat with him and his manager and set up a second experiment. Our negotiations produced the following program. He would work on the problems that came up in the feedback.

Any hint of retaliation against those who gave him the feedback would not be tolerated. After six months, once he discovered what he *could not* do, two things would happen. His supervisor would provide some coaching and counseling in the supervisory areas in which he was having difficulty and the company would provide a cost-effective in-house training program to help him deal with his deficiencies. The in-house training program focused on the key dimensions of the performance management system and the basic communication skills needed to use the system well. However, once the manager got a behavioral feel for these skills, he was told that the only way that he was going to make them second nature was by intentionally using them every day. It took him about a year to improve substantially, but he did most of the work. In the meantime his direct reports no longer suffered the fate of the damned. Furthermore, he still produced excellent business results.

Crossing Borders: Adding Value Abroad

These models are able to "cross borders." Companies and institutions in Africa, Europe, Japan, Southeast Asia, the Middle East, New Zealand, and Australia have adapted them to their own cultures. A number of people have secured jobs by using Model A to outline what they might contribute to the institution offering the position. For instance, a woman in Australia says that she got her current job because, when asked what she would do with the social service agency in question were she to become its director, she answered in terms of Model A. That is, she started with ideas on strategy, moved on to operations, and ended up with a few ideas on what kind of leadership she believed was needed in the agency. Some Japanese managers have used Model B not only to facilitate change but also to serve as a coaching-counseling process. A consultant in Africa used Model B to get farmers involved in designing a new crop management system. Because the farmers had a say in the design, they were more likely to use the system in their fields.

An agricultural scientist in the Philippines used Model B in two ways in a pest management program. After renaming it Goal-Oriented Program Planning, he used it first in a seminar with pest management scientists and technicians in Thailand. He got them to develop the current scenario (what farmers know and do in pest management) and the preferred scenario (what farmers should know and do in pest management) and in "getting there" (determining the kinds of training and development programs that would help farmers move from the current to the preferred scenario. This led to a new program aimed at helping farmers become more knowledgeable about pest management, change outmoded beliefs and attitudes, and update pest control practices. Later on a simpler version of Model B was used with farmer groups. As in the African example, the scientists came to realize that education, training, and development programs work best when the farmers get to participate. So Model B was turned into a participatory process. Working from a shared planning process helped both groups achieve their goals. These cases are not so much testimonials to the validity of these models but rather validations of the basic human common sense embedded in their structures.

There is a shadow side to businesses and institutions throughout the world. The major Model C categories are valid across nationalities, but the shadow side realities within the categories are not the same in Osaka as they are in Ottawa. I sat once in the office of one of the agricultural ministers in Ankara on a mission for an international agricultural research center. While the cultural practices were different, the shadow side was there, with a few local twists. Without ever saying so explicitly and without ever ceasing to smile, the minister told me to tell my clients back at the center that the decision concerning the location of an agricultural pilot project would not be changed. As in countries across the world, agricultural practices were to cede to political priorities.

Targets for the Shared Models Approach

So far, companies and institutions themselves have been targeted as the major beneficiaries of the shared models approach. However, two other enterprises whose mission includes, directly or indirectly, helping companies and institutions improve and prosper are also targets of the messages of this book: business schools and management consulting firms.

Business Schools

While it is not useful to engage in business school bashing, it cannot be denied that business schools, like most other institutions, face a wide range of challenges. Competition for students is growing. There is no universally accepted set of standards for professional excellence in these schools, since fewer than three hundred of some seven hundred business schools have been accredited by the American Assembly of Collegiate Schools of Business. In 1992 the U.S. Department of Education gave its approval to the Association of Collegiate Business Schools and Programs to accredit business schools. This is a sign of an industry in turmoil. This rival group, claiming that the American Assembly was too elitist, narrow, and traditional, accredits two-year undergraduate business programs in addition to four-year and graduate programs.

Critics of the schools abound and a typical criticism sounds like this: "Many consider business scholarship irrelevant and deliberately recondite; books and articles complain that business executives and business professors have little in common and communicate infrequently. Although authors have proposed inventive schemes to unite these estranged parties, little evidence of reconciliation exists. In fact, cooperation between the two groups has been so unusual that their collaboration at Duke University made national newspaper headlines" (Oviatt & Miller, 1989, p. 304).

Peter Drucker, for years one of the major management pundits in the United States, has prided himself on acting as a goad to business schools for the past thirty years. Claiming that management is a practice rather than a science, he finds the schools too abstract and wants academics to get their hands dirty in the marketplace. In the schools there is too much focus on financial, accounting, and analytic skills. While essential, these skills are only a part of the business and management skills required.

Studies show that many companies, echoing Drucker's criticisms, are dissatisfied with the products business schools are turning out. For instance, the conclusion of one study (Linden, Brennan, & Lane, 1992) was that MBA graduates lacked the practical skills needed to manage in the real world, knew little about such essentials as quality in manufacturing or managing in global markets, and lacked the kind of leadership skills needed to deal with the more diverse workforces of today's flatter organizations. While competitors to business schools are few, there are some interesting trends. Larger businesses themselves are training people in the management skills needed for that business—Amoco, IBM, General Electric, Walmart, and Xerox, to name just a few. In 1992 Motorola invited teachers from business and engineering schools to attend sessions at Motorola University to see how it teaches quality. However, participants were accepted only from schools that agreed to apply TQM methods to their own inefficient administrative systems.

Some of the most trenchant criticism comes from within the ranks of the schools themselves—a positive sign. There is a great deal of debate among the schools as to what their mission, goals, and curriculum should be. Harvard's Kaplan, in addressing the 1992 annual meeting of the American Assembly of Collegiate Schools of Business, claimed that in some areas of business, twenty to twenty-five years of business school research has produced little or no fundamental knowledge relevant for managing contemporary or future businesses. He reported that he searched through one year's worth of journals dealing with operations management and found no articles on quality. It seems that the topic is not scientific enough. Things like customer service, no matter how important they are to companies, are ignored because they are too "soft." The CEO of one successful company once said to me, "The soft things are the hard things for us in two ways. We find them hard to do and often they are precisely the things we need to do to get hard results." However, some of the "touchy-feely" courses, currently being adopted by some business schools, do not provide the needed "soft" skills. Some of these programs are neither derived from nor linked to the business. Managing culture and dealing with internal politics are soft skills, but they seldom find their way into the classroom. So-called executive programs often deal with the "softer" skills such as coaching and counseling. But at that point in a manager's life such skills are remedial.

While general management is one of the three most popular "majors" in business school, there are still no overarching set of frameworks, models, methods, and skills that constitute some kind of core curriculum for general managers-to-be. Even this specialty focuses heavily on finance, accounting, and analysis. It is not clear that the elective system in graduate programs as presently constituted serves the education and training of managers well. Choosing a bit of this and a bit of that does not provide a comprehensive managerial framework. Models A, B, and C, or some form of them, provide a comprehensive framework for graduate school curricula. Then, even if students specialize in one area of the framework, let us say operations management, its relationships to other areas would be clear. Students who specialize can also see what package of general management models and skills they will need to complement their area of specialization.

We often divide people into two camps — the theoretician-researcher on one side, the practitioner on the other — in this case, the business school professor and the manager. There is a third possibility — the "translator." Translators are professionals who, using a very critical eye, stay in touch with both the best of theory and research and everyday managerial practice. Then, because they constantly interact with practitioners and understand their needs, they translate critical findings in theory and research into pragmatic models, methods, and skills that practitioners, in this case managers, can use in their everyday lives. When Drucker urges business school academicians to get their hands dirty, he means, at least in part, that more of them should become translators.

I believe that the shared models approach could serve as the basis for a new curriculum in undergraduate business programs. More and more companies are choosing undergraduates rather than MBAs for management development slots. They, too, need finance and accounting, but they need frameworks that help them understand the needs of the businesses and institutions within which they will manage. The sooner managers-to-be get a comprehensive and integrated picture of what it means to manage, supervise, and lead, the better. A new approach in undergraduate business programs would also put pressure on graduate business schools to reform their curricula.

Consulting Firms

Business Week (1992) reviewed a number of business gurus and their contributions to management, both as developers of models and as consultants. While their contributions are impressive — the learning organization, business process reengineering, core competencies, organizational architecture, time-based competition, high-performance involvement, high-performance work systems, market-focused molecular organizations, the management of discontinuous change — I am sure that as consultants these thought leaders use comprehensive frameworks to assess the needs of their clients. They are not there merely to sell their elixirs. Companies and institutions can use frameworks like Models A, B, and C to organize and evaluate the relevance of new approaches to management, while consulting firms can use these models to provide focus and direction for their business. I continually use these frameworks to help me understand clients in terms of both their stated and unstated needs. When shared with clients, comprehensive frameworks help them understand themselves better and identify blind spots.

Managers can also use these models to prevent consultants from becoming one-track fixers. Many individual consultants and consulting firms have their own specialties. I recall one consultant whose specialty was team building. When he was asked to help a company assess its needs, he usually discovered that they needed team building. Let the buyer beware of the overspecialized consultant. Large consulting firms, too, have their specialties. Take a firm that specializes in organizational structure. Such a company needs a framework that includes both prestructure and poststructure considerations. That is, the company needs to understand the business the structure is to serve and to provide guidelines for client managers on how to make a new structure work. In short, even a consulting firm that specializes in one aspect of business and organizational life needs a comprehensive model of business and organizational effectiveness to deliver its specialty effectively.

Picture a scene slightly different from the one with which Chapter One opened. You drive up to a second bridge in an unfamiliar area of the country. Once more you have some concerns about how safe the bridge might be. A woman is standing next to the bridge, so you roll down the window and ask her what she thinks. Like the man at the other bridge, she says that she will give you the data and let you decide for yourself. She goes on to say, "This bridge was designed, engineered, constructed, and is currently being maintained by an engineering, construction, and maintenance firm all of whose professionals have all been selected, trained, and developed in the same way as managers in companies that have adopted both a shared models of management approach and a socialization/training process to make sure that their managers have the requisite skills to deliver the goods." Now would you cross that bridge?

References

Argyris, C. (1977, September–October). Double-loop learning in organizations. *Harvard Business Review,* pp. 115–125.

Argyris, C. (1986, September–October). Skilled incompetence. *Harvard Business Review,* pp. 74–79.

Argyris, C. (1990). *Overcoming organizational defenses.* Boston: Allyn & Bacon.

Argyris, C. (1991, May–June). Teaching smart people how to learn. *Harvard Business Review,* pp. 99–109.

Block, P. (1987). *The empowered manager: Positive political skills at work.* San Francisco: Jossey-Bass.

Burns, J. M. (1978). *Leadership.* New York: HarperCollins.

Carkhuff, R. R. (1974). *Cry twice! From custody to treatment: The story of institutional change.* Amherst, MA: Human Resource Development Press.

The checkoff. (1991, October 8). *Wall Street Journal,* p. A1.

Chew, W. B., Leonard-Barton, D., & Bohn, R. E. (1991, Spring). Beating Murphy's Law. *Sloan Management Review,* pp. 5–16.

Denny, W., & Bros. (1932). *Denny Dumbarton.* London: E. J. Burrow.

Egan, G. (1988). *Change agent skills B: Managing innovation and change.* San Diego: Pfeiffer.

Egan, G. (1990a). *The skilled helper.* Pacific Grove, CA: Brooks/Cole.

Egan, G. (1990b). *Exercises in helping skills.* Pacific Grove, CA: Brooks/Cole.

Egan, G., & McGourty, R. in press. *Taking the pulse: A quick audit of business, organizational, managerial, and leadership effectiveness.*

Eisenstein, P. A. (1991, September 29). Chicago challenging Atlanta in productivity world series. *Chicago Tribune,* Section 17, 8–9.

Eisenstodt, G. (1991, July 22). Bullies on the farm. *Forbes,* pp. 84–85.

Flint, J. (1991, February 4). Banzai with a Georgia accent. *Forbes,* pp. 58–62.

de Geus, A. P. (1988, March–April). Planning as learning. *Harvard Business Review,* pp. 70–74.

Goffman, E. (1967). *Interaction ritual: Essays on face-to-face behavior.* Garden City, NY: Anchor Books.

Hall, D., & Pedler, M. (1989). *Creating good business through the learning company.* Doncaster, U.K.: David Hall Partnership.

Hayes, R. H., & Abernathy, W. J. (1980, July–August). Managing our way to economic decline. *Harvard Business Review,* pp. 67–87.

Hayes, R. H., Wheelwright, S. C., & Clark, K. B. (1988). *Dynamic manufacturing: Creating the learning organization.* New York: Free Press.

Kanter, R. M. (1983). *Change masters: Innovation for productivity in the American corporation.* New York: Simon & Schuster.

Kotter, J. P. (1982, November–December). What effective managers really do. *Harvard Business Review,* pp. 156–167.

Linden, D. W., Brennan, J., & Lane, R. (1992, January 20). Another boom ends. *Forbes,* pp. 76–80.

Management's new gurus. (1992, August 31). *Business Week,* pp. 44–52.

McCann, J. E. (1991). Design principles for an innovating company. *Academy of Management Executive, 5*(2), 76–93.

Morgan, G. (1986). *Images of Organization.* Newbury Park, CA: Sage.

Oviatt, B. M., & Miller, W. D. (1989). Irrelevance, intransigence, and business professors. *The Academy of Management Executive, 3,* 304–312.

Pascale, R. (1990). *Managing on the edge: How the smartest companies use conflict to stay ahead.* New York: Simon & Schuster.

Pearson, A. E. (1992, May–June). Corporate redemption and the seven deadly sins. *Harvard Business Review,* pp. 65–75.

Peters, T. (1987). *Thriving on chaos.* New York: Knopf.

Peters, T. J., & Waterman, R. W., Jr. (1982). *In search of excellence.* New York: HarperCollins.

Porras, J. I. (1987). *Stream analysis: A powerful way to diagnose and manage organizational change.* Reading, MA: Addison-Wesley.

Schrage, M. (1991, September 9). Prototypes: Building blocks for entrepreneurs. *Wall Street Journal,* p. A10.

Senge, P. M. (1990a). *The fifth discipline.* New York: Doubleday.

Senge, P. M. (1990b, Fall). The leader's new work: Building learning organizations. *Sloan Management Review,* pp. 7–23.

Snyder, C. R., Higgins, R. L., & Stucky, R. J. (1983). *Excuses: Masquerades in search of grace.* New York: Wiley.

Stata, R. (1989, Spring). Organization learning—The key to management innovation. *Sloan Management Review,* pp. 63–74.

Weick, K. E. (1979). *The social psychology of organizing* (2nd ed.). Reading, MA: Addison-Wesley.

What happened to advertising? (1991, September 23). *Business Week,* pp. 66–72.

White, J. B. (1991, September 9). Japanese auto makers help U.S. suppliers become more efficient. *Wall Street Journal,* pp. A1, A8.

Wriston, W. (1986). *Risk and other four-letter words.* New York: HarperCollins.

Yasuda, Y. (1991). *40 years, 20 million ideas.* Cambridge, MA: Productivity Press.

Index